William Shakespeare's
The Winter Tale
In Plain and Simple English

BookCaps™ Study Guides
www.swipespeare.com

Table of Contents

About This Series

The "Classic Retold" series started as a way of telling classics for the modern reader—being careful to preserve the themes and integrity of the original. Whether you want to understand Shakespeare a little more or are trying to get a better grasps of the Greek classics, there is a book waiting for you!

The series is expanding every month. Visit BookCaps.com to see all the books in the series, and while you are there join the Facebook page, so you are first to know when a new book comes out.

Characters

LEONTES, King of Sicilia
MAMILLIUS, his son
CAMILLO, Sicilian Lord
ANTIGONUS, Sicilian Lord
CLEOMENES, Sicilian Lord
DION, Sicilian Lord
Other Sicilian Lords.
Sicilian Gentlemen.
Officers of a Court of Judicature
POLIXENES, King of Bohemia
FLORIZEL, his son
ARCHIDAMUS, a Bohemian Lord
A Mariner
Gaoler
An Old Shepherd, reputed father of Perdita
CLOWN, his son
Servant to the Old Shepherd
AUTOLYCUS, a rogue
TIME, as Chorus
HERMIONE, Queen to Leontes
PERDITA, daughter to Leontes and Hermione
PAULINA, wife to Antigonus
EMILIA, a lady attending on the Queen
Other Ladies, attending on the Queen
MOPSA, shepherdess
DORCAS, shepherdess
Lords, Ladies, and Attendants
Satyrs for a Dance
Shepherds, Shepherdesses, Guards, &c.

SCENE: Sometimes in Sicilia; sometimes in Bohemia.

Comparative Version

Act 1

Scene 1

SCENE I. Antechamber in LEONTES' palace.

Enter CAMILLO and ARCHIDAMUS

ARCHIDAMUS
If you shall chance, Camillo, to visit Bohemia, on
the like occasion whereon my services are now on
foot, you shall see, as I have said, great
difference betwixt our Bohemia and your Sicilia.

If you happen, Camillo, to visit Bohemia, on
the same sort of mission as I am undertaking,
you will see, as I said, a great
difference between our Bohemia and your Sicily.

CAMILLO
I think, this coming summer, the King of Sicilia
means to pay Bohemia the visitation which he justly
owes him.

I think, this coming summer, the King of Sicily
intends to make the return visit to Bohemia which he
is due.

ARCHIDAMUS
Wherein our entertainment shall shame us; we will
be
justified in our loves; for indeed--

When he does our entertainment will embarrass us;
we will
make up for it with our love; for in fact–

CAMILLO
Beseech you,--

Please, now–

ARCHIDAMUS
Verily, I speak it in the freedom of my knowledge:
we cannot with such magnificence, in so rare--I
know
not what to say. We will give you sleepy drinks,

that your senses, unintelligent of our insufficience,

may, though they cannot praise us, as little accuse
us.

Honestly, I know what I'm talking about:
we cannot compete with such magnificence, such
rarities–I don't
know what to say. We shall have to drug your
drinks,
so that your senses, being unable to see our
inadequacies,
might, although they couldn't praise us, not criticise
us.

CAMILLO
You pay a great deal too dear for what's given
freely.

You're trying too hard for something we'd be
delighted to give.

ARCHIDAMUS
Believe me, I speak as my understanding instructs
me
and as mine honesty puts it to utterance.

Believe me, I'm saying what I know,

in the manner which honesty compels me.

CAMILLO

Sicilia cannot show himself over-kind to Bohemia.
They were trained together in their childhoods; and
there rooted betwixt them then such an affection,
which cannot choose but branch now. Since their
more mature dignities and royal necessities made
separation of their society, their encounters,
though not personal, have been royally attorneyed
with interchange of gifts, letters, loving
embassies; that they have seemed to be together,

though absent, shook hands, as over a vast, and

embraced, as it were, from the ends of opposed
winds. The heavens continue their loves!

*Sicily cannot treat Bohemia with enough kindness.
They were educated together as children; and
such affection grew up between them
that they are now inseparable. Since the
responsibilities of adulthood and their royal duties
forced them to live apart, their meetings,
though not personal, have been carried out by
substitutes, with a royal exchange of gifts, letters,
loving messages; so it seemed as though they were
together,
though apart; as if they shook hands over a great
distance;
and embraced, as it were, from far corners
of the earth. May the gods keep them so affectionate!*

ARCHIDAMUS
I think there is not in the world either malice or
matter to alter it. You have an unspeakable
comfort of your young prince Mamillius: it is a

gentleman of the greatest promise that ever came
into my note.

*I don't think that there is any evil or
subject in the world that could alter it. You are
incredibly lucky to have your young Prince
Mamillius:
he's got more promise than any gentleman who ever
came to my attention.*

CAMILLO
I very well agree with you in the hopes of him: it
is a gallant child; one that indeed physics the
subject, makes old hearts fresh: they that went on
crutches ere he was born desire yet their life to

see him a man.

*I certainly agree with you about his potential: he
is a gallant child; he's one who cheers the soul,
livens up old hearts: people who were
already walking with sticks before he was born
want to live long enough to
see him grow up to be a man.*

ARCHIDAMUS
Would they else be content to die?

Would they have been happy to die otherwise?

CAMILLO
Yes; if there were no other excuse why they should
desire to live.

Yes; if there was no other reason for living.

ARCHIDAMUS
If the king had no son, they would desire to live
on crutches till he had one.

*If the king didn't have a son, they would want to live,
sticks and all, until he had one.*

Scene 2

SCENE II. A room of state in the same.

Enter LEONTES, HERMIONE, MAMILLIUS, POLIXENES, CAMILLO, and Attendants

POLIXENES
Nine changes of the watery star hath been
The shepherd's note since we have left our throne
Without a burthen: time as long again
Would be find up, my brother, with our thanks;
And yet we should, for perpetuity,
Go hence in debt: and therefore, like a cipher,
Yet standing in rich place, I multiply
With one 'We thank you' many thousands moe
That go before it.

Nine months have passed since
I left my throne
empty: it would take as much time again,
my brother, to thank you properly,
and I would still be in your debt
forever: so one 'thank you' must act
like a zero added to the end of a number,
worthless in itself but multiplying all the
thousands which went before it.

LEONTES
Stay your thanks a while;
And pay them when you part.

Don't thank me yet;
do that when you leave.

POLIXENES
Sir, that's to-morrow.
I am question'd by my fears, of what may chance
Or breed upon our absence; that may blow
No sneaping winds at home, to make us say

'This is put forth too truly:' besides, I have stay'd
To tire your royalty.

Sir, I'm leaving tomorrow.
I am worried by thoughts of what might happen,
or be brewing, while I'm away; I hope
there are no ill winds blowing at home, that would
make me say,
"My fears were justified." Anyway, I've outstayed
your royal welcome.

LEONTES
We are tougher, brother,
Than you can put us to't.

I can put up with you
for far longer, brother.

POLIXENES
No longer stay.

I can't stay any longer.

LEONTES
One seven-night longer.

Just another week.

POLIXENES
Very sooth, to-morrow.

No, I must go tomorrow.

LEONTES
We'll part the time between's then; and in that
I'll no gainsaying.

We'll split the difference, and that's
my last word on the matter.

POLIXENES

Press me not, beseech you, so.
There is no tongue that moves, none, none i' the world,
So soon as yours could win me: so it should now,
Were there necessity in your request, although
'Twere needful I denied it. My affairs
Do even drag me homeward: which to hinder
Were in your love a whip to me; my stay
To you a charge and trouble: to save both,
Farewell, our brother.

Please don't tempt me.
There is nobody in the world who could

convince me as easily as you; you would do now,
if there was any reason for your request, even
if I really ought to refuse it. My affairs
are calling me home; to stop me would be
doing me wrong, even though done out of love;
it would not do you credit for me to stay; to
prevent this I say goodbye, my brother.

LEONTES

Tongue-tied, our queen?
speak you.

Silent, my queen?
Speak.

HERMIONE

I had thought, sir, to have held my peace until
You have drawn oaths from him not to stay. You, sir,
Charge him too coldly. Tell him, you are sure
All in Bohemia's well; this satisfaction
The by-gone day proclaim'd: say this to him,
He's beat from his best ward.

I was going to keep my peace until
you had made him promise to stay. You, sir,

have not done your best. Tell him, you are certain
that everything is fine in Bohemia; I had the news
from there just yesterday; tell him we've beaten
his best defence.

LEONTES

Well said, Hermione.

Well said, Hermione.

HERMIONE

To tell, he longs to see his son, were strong:

But let him say so then, and let him go;
But let him swear so, and he shall not stay,
We'll thwack him hence with distaffs.
Yet of your royal presence I'll adventure
The borrow of a week. When at Bohemia
You take my lord, I'll give him my commission
To let him there a month behind the gest
Prefix'd for's parting: yet, good deed, Leontes,
I love thee not a jar o' the clock behind
What lady-she her lord. You'll stay?

If he said he was longing to see his son, that would
be a good reason:
but if that's the case let him say so, and let him go;
but if he says he can't stay for the reason he's given
we'll drive him out of here with canes.
But I'll ask for you to stay here
an extra week. If you do then when you host
my husband in Bohemia I'll let him stay
a month longer than his allotted time, even though,
good Leontes, I don't love you a whisker less
than any other lady loves her lord. Will you stay?

POLIXENES

No, madam.

No, madam

HERMIONE

Nay, but you will?

No meaning yes?

POLIXENES
I may not, verily.

I really can't.

HERMIONE
Verily!
You put me off with limber vows; but I,
Though you would seek to unsphere the
stars with oaths,
Should yet say 'Sir, no going.' Verily,
You shall not go: a lady's 'Verily' 's
As potent as a lord's. Will you go yet?
Force me to keep you as a prisoner,
Not like a guest; so you shall pay your fees
When you depart, and save your thanks. How say
you?
My prisoner? or my guest? by your dread 'Verily,'

One of them you shall be.

Really!
You put me off with shoddy excuses; but I,
even though you're trying to swear so forcefully
that you must go,
will still say, 'Sir, don't go.' Really,
you shan't go: a lady's 'really' is just
as powerful as a lord's. Do you still say you'll go?
You'll force me to keep you as a prisoner,
Not as a guest; you'll have to pay for your keep
when you leave, never mind your thanks. What do
you say?
Will you be my prisoner, or my guest? With your
"really",
you'll be one of them.

POLIXENES
Your guest, then, madam:
To be your prisoner should import offending;

Which is for me less easy to commit
Than you to punish.

I'll be your guest then madam:
to be your prisoner would mean I would have to
commit an offence,
and that would be easier for you to punish
than for me to commit.

HERMIONE
Not your gaoler, then,
But your kind hostess. Come, I'll question you
Of my lord's tricks and yours when you were boys:

You were pretty lordings then?

So I won't be your jailer, then,
but your kind hostess. come, I want to question you
about the tricks you and my lord got up to when you
were boys:
you were pretty little lords then?

POLIXENES
We were, fair queen,
Two lads that thought there was no more behind
But such a day to-morrow as to-day,

And to be boy eternal.

We were, fair queen,
two lads who thought there was no more to come
except a tomorrow which would be the same as
today,
and that we would be boys forever.

HERMIONE
Was not my lord
The verier wag o' the two?

And wasn't my husband
the merrier of the pair?

POLIXENES
We were as twinn'd lambs that did frisk i' the sun,
And bleat the one at the other: what we changed
Was innocence for innocence; we knew not

We were like twin lambs playing in the sun,
bleating to each other: we matched
each other's innocence; we didn't know

13

The doctrine of ill-doing, nor dream'd
That any did. Had we pursued that life,

And our weak spirits ne'er been higher rear'd
With stronger blood, we should have answer'd heaven
Boldly 'not guilty;' the imposition clear'd
Hereditary ours.

HERMIONE
By this we gather
You have tripp'd since.

POLIXENES
O my most sacred lady!
Temptations have since then been born to's; for
In those unfledged days was my wife a girl;
Your precious self had then not cross'd the eyes
Of my young play-fellow.

HERMIONE
Grace to boot!
Of this make no conclusion, lest you say
Your queen and I are devils: yet go on;
The offences we have made you do we'll answer,

If you first sinn'd with us and that with us
You did continue fault and that you slipp'd not
With any but with us.

LEONTES
Is he won yet?

HERMIONE
He'll stay my lord.

LEONTES
At my request he would not.
Hermione, my dearest, thou never spokest
To better purpose.

HERMIONE
Never?

LEONTES
Never, but once.

about wrongdoing, nor dreamed that anyone else did wrong. If we had stayed in that state,
never having our weak spirits raised up through our strong ancestry, when heaven charged us
with original sin we would have boldly answered "not guilty", thinking we had never done anything wrong.

From this one might assume that you have sinned since.

O my dear lady!
Temptation has come our way since then; in those days of youth my wife was just a girl; your precious being had not then come to the eye of my young playmate.

Heaven help us!
Don't continue this argument, in case you say that your queen and I are devils: but go on; we'll take responsibility for the offences we've made you do,
if your first sin was committed with us, and your sins continued with us, and you didn't sin with anyone except us.

Has he given in yet?

He'll stay, my lord.

He wouldn't when I asked him.
Hermione, my dearest, you never spoke with better effect.

Never?

Never, except for one time.

HERMIONE
What! have I twice said well? when was't before?

I prithee tell me; cram's with praise, and make's
As fat as tame things: one good deed dying tongueless
Slaughters a thousand waiting upon that.
Our praises are our wages: you may ride's
With one soft kiss a thousand furlongs ere
With spur we beat an acre. But to the goal:

My last good deed was to entreat his stay:

What was my first? it has an elder sister,
Or I mistake you: O, would her name were Grace!

But once before I spoke to the purpose: when?
Nay, let me have't; I long.

What! Have I spoken well twice? When was the previous time?
Please tell me; fill me with praise, make me as fat as a farm animal: one good deed going unpraised could stop a thousand that were about to be done.
Praise is our wages: you can get us to go a thousand furlongs with one soft kiss before we'll cross a single one beaten with spurs. But to the point:
the last good thing I did was to persuade him to stay:
what was the first good thing? It has an elder sister, or I've misunderstood you: oh, I wish her name was Grace!
But once before I have said something good: when? Come on, tell me, I'm dying to hear.

LEONTES
Why, that was when
Three crabbed months had sour'd themselves to death,
Ere I could make thee open thy white hand
And clap thyself my love: then didst thou utter
'I am yours for ever.'

Why, it was when three miserable months had withered away,

before I could make you open your white hand to take mine with love: it was then that you said 'I am yours forever.'

HERMIONE
'Tis grace indeed.
Why, lo you now, I have spoke to the purpose twice:
The one for ever earn'd a royal husband;
The other for some while a friend.

So it is called Grace.
Well, look at this, I have spoken well twice: the first one earned me a royal husband for ever; the second one a friend for some time.

LEONTES
[Aside] Too hot, too hot!
To mingle friendship far is mingling bloods.
I have tremor cordis on me: my heart dances;
But not for joy; not joy. This entertainment

May a free face put on, derive a liberty
From heartiness, from bounty, fertile bosom,

And well become the agent; 't may, I grant;
But to be paddling palms and pinching fingers,

As now they are, and making practised smiles,
As in a looking-glass, and then to sigh, as 'twere
The mort o' the deer; O, that is entertainment

That's a bit too much!
If you take friendship too far it becomes sex.
I have palpitations: my heart is dancing;
but not for happiness; no not happiness. This welcome
might look innocent, might take its liberties from cordiality, from generosity, from abundant affection,
and suit the giver very well; it might, I'll grant;
but to be toying with their hands and twining their fingers,
as they now are, and making studied smiles, as if in a looking glass, and then sighing, as if they were a dying deer; oh, this is a game

15

My bosom likes not, nor my brows! Mamillius,
Art thou my boy?

MAMILLIUS
Ay, my good lord.

LEONTES
I' fecks!
Why, that's my bawcock. What, hast
smutch'd thy nose?
They say it is a copy out of mine. Come, captain,
We must be neat; not neat, but cleanly, captain:
And yet the steer, the heifer and the calf
Are all call'd neat.--Still virginalling
Upon his palm!--How now, you wanton calf!
Art thou my calf?

MAMILLIUS
Yes, if you will, my lord.

LEONTES
Thou want'st a rough pash and the shoots that I
have,
To be full like me: yet they say we are
Almost as like as eggs; women say so,
That will say anything but were they false
As o'er-dyed blacks, as wind, as waters, false

As dice are to be wish'd by one that fixes

No bourn 'twixt his and mine, yet were it true
To say this boy were like me. Come, sir page,
Look on me with your welkin eye: sweet villain!
Most dear'st! my collop! Can thy dam?--may't be?--

Affection! thy intention stabs the centre:
Thou dost make possible things not so held,
Communicatest with dreams;--how can this be?--
With what's unreal thou coactive art,
And fellow'st nothing: then 'tis very credent
Thou mayst co-join with something; and thou dost,
And that beyond commission, and I find it,
And that to the infection of my brains
And hardening of my brows.

POLIXENES
What means Sicilia?

my heart does not enjoy, nor does my head!
Mamillius, are you my boy?

Yes, my good lord.

By God!
Well, that's my good lad. What, have you
got a smudge on your nose?
They say it is identical to mine. Come, captain,
we must be neat; not just neat, but clean, captain:
after all even cattle
can be called neat. Still playing a tune
on his palm! Now then, you frisky calf!
Are you my calf?

Yes, if that's what you want, my lord.

You need a shaggy head and the horns I have

to really be like me; yet they say we are
almost as identical as eggs. Women say so,
women who will say anything. But they are
as false as re-dyed clothes, as wind, as the waters,
false
as dice are, desired by someone who makes no
distinction
between what's mine and what's his, but it is true
to say this boy is like me. Come, my lad,
look at me with your sky-blue eye. Sweet rascal!
My dearest! My flesh and blood! Can your mother?
Can it be?
Desire, you strike right to the heart of the soul.
You make possible things thought impossible,
that were only seen in dreams—how can this be?—
You are partner with the impossible,
and so nothing is impossible. Then it's very likely
that you can partner something else; and you have,
and that is beyond belief, and I have found it,
and that is what has driven me mad,
and made me a cuckold.

What does Sicily mean?

HERMIONE
He something seems unsettled.

He seems a little disturbed.

POLIXENES
How, my lord!
What cheer? how is't with you, best brother?

Hello, my lord!
What's the story? How are things with you, my
dearest brother?

HERMIONE
You look as if you held a brow of much distraction.
Are you moved, my lord?

You look as if something is bothering you.
Are you upset, my lord?

LEONTES
No, in good earnest.
How sometimes nature will betray its folly,
Its tenderness, and make itself a pastime
To harder bosoms! Looking on the lines
Of my boy's face, methoughts I did recoil
Twenty-three years, and saw myself unbreech'd,
In my green velvet coat, my dagger muzzled,
Lest it should bite its master, and so prove,
As ornaments oft do, too dangerous:
How like, methought, I then was to this kernel,
This squash, this gentleman. Mine honest friend,
Will you take eggs for money?

No, I assure you.
Sometimes perfection will show its weakness,
its tenderness, and become a plaything
for harder hearts! Looking at
my boy's face, I thought I went back
twenty-three years and saw myself as a small child,
in my green velvet coat, my dagger with a cork
on the point, in case it will should stab me, and so be
as ornaments often are, too dangerous.
I thought how similar I was then to this seed,
this unripe plant, this gentleman. My honest friend,
will you allow yourself to be conned?

MAMILLIUS
No, my lord, I'll fight.

No, my lord, I'll fight.

LEONTES
You will! why, happy man be's dole! My brother,

Are you so fond of your young prince as we
Do seem to be of ours?

You will! Well, may happiness be your future! My
brother,
are you as fond of your young prince as I
seem to be of mine?

POLIXENES
If at home, sir,
He's all my exercise, my mirth, my matter,

Now my sworn friend and then mine enemy,
My parasite, my soldier, statesman, all:
He makes a July's day short as December,
And with his varying childness cures in me
Thoughts that would thick my blood.

When I'm at home, sir,
he's everything to me, my laughter, my serious
moments,
one minute my greatest friend, and then my enemy,
my beggar, my soldier, politician, everything:
he makes a July day fly by as if it was December,
and with his childish moods he alleviates
any melancholy in me.

LEONTES
So stands this squire

That's the way it is

Officed with me: we two will walk, my lord, | with this lad and me: he and I shall walk together, my lord,

And leave you to your graver steps. Hermione, | and leave you to your adult pastimes. Hermione,
How thou lovest us, show in our brother's welcome; | show your love for me in the way you entertain our brother;

Let what is dear in Sicily be cheap: | let him have all the best things in Sicily cheap:
Next to thyself and my young rover, he's | after you and my young scamp, he
Apparent to my heart. | is the heir of my affections.

HERMIONE
If you would seek us, | If you want us,
We are yours i' the garden: shall's attend you there? | we will be in the garden: shall we meet you there?

LEONTES
To your own bents dispose you: you'll be found, | Do as you please: you will be discovered,
Be you beneath the sky. | as long as you are somewhere on earth.

Aside | [Aside] I am fishing now,
I am angling now,
Though you perceive me not how I give line. | although you can't see my cunning technique.
Go to, go to! | Go on, go on!
How she holds up the neb, the bill to him! | Look at how she's holding her mouth up towards him!

And arms her with the boldness of a wife | Look how she's taking advantage
To her allowing husband! | of her husband's permissiveness!

Exeunt POLIXENES, HERMIONE, and Attendants
Gone already! | Gone already!
Inch-thick, knee-deep, o'er head and | I'm deep into my betrayal!
ears a fork'd one! | Go and play, boy, play: your mother is playing and I
Go, play, boy, play: thy mother plays, and I | am playing too—but the part I'm playing is so disgraceful

Play too, but so disgraced a part, whose issue | that I shall be hissed for it to the grave. Contempt and booing

Will hiss me to my grave: contempt and clamour | will be my funeral bell. Go and play, boy, play. There have been,

Will be my knell. Go, play, boy, play. | unless I am much mistaken, cuckolds before now;
There have been, | and there is many a man who, even right now,
Or I am much deceived, cuckolds ere now; | now, as I'm speaking, is holding his wife's hands,
And many a man there is, even at this present, | hardly suspecting that she has been diverted while he's away,

Now while I speak this, holds his wife by the arm, | and that his next door neighbour has been fishing in his pond,

That little thinks she has been sluiced in's absence | his smiling next door neighbour. I suppose it's a comforting thought

And his pond fish'd by his next neighbour, by | to know that other men have their property broken into

Sir Smile, his neighbour: nay, there's comfort in't | against their will, as I do. If everyone who had

Whiles other men have gates and those gates open'd, *a cheating wife was to despair, a tenth of mankind*
As mine, against their will. Should all despair *would hang themselves. There's no cure for it:*
That have revolted wives, the tenth of mankind *it's influenced by a lusty planet that ruins everything*
Would hang themselves. Physic for't there is none; *when it's in the ascendant; and you can be sure it's powerful*

It is a bawdy planet, that will strike *in the east, west, north and south. It can be seen*
Where 'tis predominant; and 'tis powerful, think it, *that there is no way to blockade a womb. Be certain:*
From east, west, north and south: be it concluded, *it will let the enemy be in and out*
No barricado for a belly; know't; *with all his bags and baggage. Many thousands of us*

It will let in and out the enemy *suffer like this and don't know about it. What, boy?*
With bag and baggage: many thousand on's
Have the disease, and feel't not. How now, boy!

MAMILLIUS
I am like you, they say.   *They say I am like you.*

LEONTES
Why, that's some comfort. What, Camillo there?   *Well, that's some comfort. Hello, is that Camillo there?*

CAMILLO
Ay, my good lord.   *Yes, my good lord.*

LEONTES
Go play, Mamillius; thou'rt an honest man.   *Go and play, Mamillius; you're a good man.*

Exit MAMILLIUS
Camillo, this great sir will yet stay longer.   *Camillo, this great lord will stay with us a little while longer.*

CAMILLO
You had much ado to make his anchor hold: *You made a great effort to anchor him:*
When you cast out, it still came home.   *you threw it out, but it still came back.*

LEONTES
Didst note it?   *You noticed it?*

CAMILLO
He would not stay at your petitions: made   *He wouldn't stay when you asked him:*
His business more material.   *he said he had other business.*

LEONTES
Didst perceive it?   *You noticed that?*

Aside
They're here with me already, whispering, rounding   *They're here with me already, whispering, passing on*

'Sicilia is a so-forth:' 'tis far gone,

When I shall gust it last. How came't, Camillo,

That he did stay?

CAMILLO
At the good queen's entreaty.

LEONTES
At the queen's be't: 'good' should be pertinent
But, so it is, it is not. Was this taken
By any understanding pate but thine?
For thy conceit is soaking, will draw in
More than the common blocks: not noted, is't,

But of the finer natures? by some severals
Of head-piece extraordinary? lower messes
Perchance are to this business purblind? say.

CAMILLO
Business, my lord! I think most understand
Bohemia stays here longer.

LEONTES
Ha!

CAMILLO
Stays here longer.

LEONTES
Ay, but why?

CAMILLO
To satisfy your highness and the entreaties
Of our most gracious mistress.

LEONTES
Satisfy!
The entreaties of your mistress! satisfy!
Let that suffice. I have trusted thee, Camillo,
With all the nearest things to my heart, as well
My chamber-councils, wherein, priest-like, thou
Hast cleansed my bosom, I from thee departed
Thy penitent reform'd: but we have been
Deceived in thy integrity, deceived
In that which seems so.

'Sicily is a such and such:' the business is much advanced,
and I'm the last to know. How did it happen, Camillo,
that he ended up staying?

Because the good queen begged him.

The queen begged him: "good" should be applicable
but as things stand it is not. Was this noticed
by any observant mind apart from yours?
For you pick things up quickly, you notice
more than the common blockheads: it isn't noticed, is it,
except by the keener minds? By a few people
with excellent brains? The mob
are quite blind to this business, aren't they? Tell me.

Business, my lord! I think most people understand
that Bohemia will be staying here for longer.

Ha!

He stays here longer.

Yes, but why?

To please your Highness and the pleas
of our most gracious mistress.

Satisfy!
The pleas of your mistress! Satisfy!
Let that be enough. I have trusted you, Camillo,
with all my innermost secrets, my
intimate confidences, and like a priest
you have eased my burden, I left you
like a reformed sinner: but I have been
misled as to your honesty, tricked
by what you seemed to be.

CAMILLO
Be it forbid, my lord!

Heaven forbid, my lord!

LEONTES
To bide upon't, thou art not honest, or,
If thou inclinest that way, thou art a coward,
Which hoxes honesty behind, restraining
From course required; or else thou must be counted
A servant grafted in my serious trust
And therein negligent; or else a fool
That seest a game play'd home, the rich stake drawn,

And takest it all for jest.

To explain, you are not honest, or,
if you are, you are a coward,
which holds honesty back, preventing it taking
the necessary action; either you are
my trusted servant, in which case
you are negligent; or else you're a fool,
who sees a game played to a finish, a rich prize
won,
and thinks it's all in fun.

CAMILLO
My gracious lord,
I may be negligent, foolish and fearful;
In every one of these no man is free,
But that his negligence, his folly, fear,
Among the infinite doings of the world,
Sometime puts forth. In your affairs, my lord,

If ever I were wilful-negligent,
It was my folly; if industriously
I play'd the fool, it was my negligence,
Not weighing well the end; if ever fearful
To do a thing, where I the issue doubted,
Where of the execution did cry out
Against the non-performance, 'twas a fear
Which oft infects the wisest: these, my lord,
Are such allow'd infirmities that honesty
Is never free of. But, beseech your grace,
Be plainer with me; let me know my trespass
By its own visage: if I then deny it,
'Tis none of mine.

My gracious lord,
I may be negligent, stupid and cowardly:
no man can ever be completely free of these things,
and amidst all the many happenings of the world
his negligence, stupidity and cowardice
will sometimes appear. In doing your business, my
lord,
if I was ever deliberately negligent
it was through stupidity; if in my work
I played the fool, it was negligent of me,
not thinking of the outcome; if I was ever afraid
to do anything because I feared the outcome,
when it was proved right once done, that's a fear
which often takes hold of the wisest. My lord,
these are common weaknesses that an honest man
can never be free of. But, I beg your grace,
be straight with me, let me know exactly
what I've done wrong; if I then deny it,
you can be sure I didn't do it.

LEONTES
Ha' not you seen, Camillo,--
But that's past doubt, you have, or your eye-glass
Is thicker than a cuckold's horn,--or heard,--
For to a vision so apparent rumour
Cannot be mute,--or thought,--for cogitation
Resides not in that man that does not think,--
My wife is slippery? If thou wilt confess,
Or else be impudently negative,
To have nor eyes nor ears nor thought, then say
My wife's a hobby-horse, deserves a name
As rank as any flax-wench that puts to

Haven't you seen, Camillo--
but you must have done, if your glasses
are thinner than a cuckold's horn--or heard--
for with your sharp ears you must pick up
the rumours--or thought--for speculation
doesn't happen in the mind of the unthinking man--
that's my wife is unfaithful? If you will admit it--
because otherwise you would have to boldly deny
things that you can see, hear and think--then say
my wife's a tart, deserving a reputation
as bad as any flighty girl who puts out

Before her troth-plight: say't and justify't.

before she is married: say it and explain it.

CAMILLO
I would not be a stander-by to hear
My sovereign mistress clouded so, without
My present vengeance taken: 'shrew my heart,
You never spoke what did become you less
Than this; which to reiterate were sin
As deep as that, though true.

*I won't stand by to listen to
my royal mistress being so insulted
without responding: damn me sir,
you never let yourself down so badly
as you do in saying this; repeating it
is a sin as bad as the one you're describing.*

LEONTES
Is whispering nothing?
Is leaning cheek to cheek? is meeting noses?
Kissing with inside lip? stopping the career
Of laughing with a sigh?--a note infallible
Of breaking honesty--horsing foot on foot?
Skulking in corners? wishing clocks more swift?
Hours, minutes? noon, midnight? and all eyes

Blind with the pin and web but theirs, theirs only,

That would unseen be wicked? is this nothing?

Why, then the world and all that's in't is nothing;
The covering sky is nothing; Bohemia nothing;
My wife is nothing; nor nothing have these nothings,
If this be nothing.

*Does whispering mean nothing?
Does leaning cheek to cheek? Does rubbing noses?
Kissing on the lips? Breaking off from laughing
to sigh?–a sure sign
of dishonesty. Playing footsie?
Hiding in corners? Wishing time would speed up?
Wishing hours were minutes? That noon was
midnight?
That all eyes were covered with cataracts except
theirs,only theirs,
so they could be with cute undetected–is this
nothing?
Well, then the world and everything in it is nothing;
the sky above is nothing; Bohemia is nothing;
my wife is nothing; and there is nothing in these
nothings,
if this is nothing.*

CAMILLO
Good my lord, be cured
Of this diseased opinion, and betimes;
For 'tis most dangerous.

*My good lord, drop
this horrible thought, and quickly;
it is dangerous.*

LEONTES
Say it be, 'tis true.

Say I'm right, it's true.

CAMILLO
No, no, my lord.

No, no, my lord.

LEONTES
It is; you lie, you lie:
I say thou liest, Camillo, and I hate thee,
Pronounce thee a gross lout, a mindless slave,
Or else a hovering temporizer, that
Canst with thine eyes at once see good and evil,
Inclining to them both: were my wife's liver

*It is; you lie, you lie:
I say you are lying, Camillo, and I hate you,
call you a gross lout, a mindless slave,
unless you are a two-faced waverer, who
can see both good and evil at the same time
and treat them both the same: if my wife's liver*

Original	Modern
Infected as her life, she would not live The running of one glass.	*was as diseased as her lifestyle, she would not live another hour.*
CAMILLO Who does infect her?	*Who has given her this disease?*
LEONTES Why, he that wears her like a medal, hanging About his neck, Bohemia: who, if I Had servants true about me, that bare eyes To see alike mine honour as their profits, Their own particular thrifts, they would do that Which should undo more doing: ay, and thou, His cupbearer,--whom I from meaner form Have benched and reared to worship, who mayst see Plainly as heaven sees earth and earth sees heaven, How I am galled,--mightst bespice a cup, To give mine enemy a lasting wink; Which draught to me were cordial.	*Why, the one who wears her like a medal, hanging round his neck, Bohemia: the one who, if I had loyal servants, who had an eye to my honour as well as their own profits, their own benefit, they would do something to stop his carrying on: yes, and you, his cupbearer—whom I promoted from a low position to be in my service, who can see, as plainly as heaven sees earth and vice versa, how I am tormented—might slip something in a cup, to give my enemy a permanent sleep. That would be tasty drink to me.*
CAMILLO Sir, my lord, I could do this, and that with no rash potion, But with a lingering dram that should not work Maliciously like poison: but I cannot Believe this crack to be in my dread mistress, So sovereignly being honourable. I have loved thee,--	*Sir, my lord, I could do this, and not with some harsh potion but with a sweet tasting drop that would not work horribly like poison: but I cannot believe that my awe-inspiring mistress has such a flaw, being of such royal honour. I have loved you–*
LEONTES Make that thy question, and go rot! Dost think I am so muddy, so unsettled, To appoint myself in this vexation, sully The purity and whiteness of my sheets, Which to preserve is sleep, which being spotted Is goads, thorns, nettles, tails of wasps, Give scandal to the blood o' the prince my son, Who I do think is mine and love as mine, Without ripe moving to't? Would I do this? Could man so blench?	*If you doubt it, then go to hell! Do you think I am so filthy, so mad, to lay this burden on myself, dirty the purity and whiteness of my sheets, which if clean let me sleep, if dirty then they become a bed of nails, call into question the paternity of my son the prince, who I think is mine and love as mine, unless I had good reason for it? Would I do this? Could any man be so far wrong?*
CAMILLO I must believe you, sir: I do; and will fetch off Bohemia for't; Provided that, when he's removed, your highness Will take again your queen as yours at first, Even for your son's sake; and thereby for sealing	*I must believe you, sir: I do; and I will kill Bohemia for it; provided that, once he's gone, your Highness will take your queen back into your arms, at least for your son's sake; and in that way*

The injury of tongues in courts and kingdoms
Known and allied to yours.

LEONTES
Thou dost advise me
Even so as I mine own course have set down:
I'll give no blemish to her honour, none.

CAMILLO
My lord,
Go then; and with a countenance as clear
As friendship wears at feasts, keep with Bohemia

And with your queen. I am his cupbearer:
If from me he have wholesome beverage,
Account me not your servant.

LEONTES
This is all:
Do't and thou hast the one half of my heart;
Do't not, thou split'st thine own.

CAMILLO
I'll do't, my lord.

LEONTES
I will seem friendly, as thou hast advised me.

Exit

CAMILLO
O miserable lady! But, for me,
What case stand I in? I must be the poisoner
Of good Polixenes; and my ground to do't
Is the obedience to a master, one
Who in rebellion with himself will have
All that are his so too. To do this deed,
Promotion follows. If I could find example
Of thousands that had struck anointed kings
And flourish'd after, I'ld not do't; but since

Nor brass nor stone nor parchment bears not one,

Let villany itself forswear't. I must
Forsake the court: to do't, or no, is certain
To me a break-neck. Happy star, reign now!

Here comes Bohemia.

---

*you will stop the gossip in the courts and kingdoms
that are known and allied to yours.*

*This advice of yours
is exactly what I was going to do:
I will not put any stain on her honour, none.*

*Go then my lord,
and with an open smiling face
such as a friend shows on holiday, stay with
Bohemia
and your queen. I am his cupbearer:
if he gets a healthy drink from me,
you can say I am not your servant.*

*This is the deal:
do it and you have won half of my heart;
don't do it, and your own will be torn.*

I'll do it, my lord.

I'll pretend to be friendly, as you have advised me.

*Oh unfortunate lady! But, as for me,
what sort of position am I in? I must poison
good Polixenes, and my reason for it
is to obey my master, who,
being tormented in his mind
wants all his household to be so too. If I do this,
I will get advancement. Even if I could find examples
of thousands who had fought against chosen kings
and prospered afterwards, I would not do it; but
since
neither brass nor stone nor parchment shows a
single one,
let the evil stop. I must
leave the court: to do it or not, either way
I'm certain to be hanged. Guardian angel, help me
now!
Here comes Bohemia.*

Re-enter POLIXENES

POLIXENES
This is strange: methinks
My favour here begins to warp. Not speak?
Good day, Camillo.

This is strange: I feel
that my welcome here has cooled. Not talking?
Good day, Camillo.

CAMILLO
Hail, most royal sir!

Greetings, most royal sir!

POLIXENES
What is the news i' the court?

What's the news in the court?

CAMILLO
None rare, my lord.

Nothing unusual, my lord.

POLIXENES
The king hath on him such a countenance
As he had lost some province and a region
Loved as he loves himself: even now I met him

With customary compliment; when he,
Wafting his eyes to the contrary and falling
A lip of much contempt, speeds from me and
So leaves me to consider what is breeding
That changeth thus his manners.

The king has got a face on him
as if he had lost some province, an area
he loved as much as he loves himself: just now I met
him
with the usual politeness; he,
rolling his eyes away and curling
his lip in contempt, sped away from me and
left me wondering what is going on
that has changed his attitude so much.

CAMILLO
I dare not know, my lord.

I wouldn't dare to guess, my lord.

POLIXENES
How! dare not! do not. Do you know, and dare not
Be intelligent to me? 'tis thereabouts;
For, to yourself, what you do know, you must.
And cannot say, you dare not. Good Camillo,

Your changed complexions are to me a mirror
Which shows me mine changed too; for I must be
A party in this alteration, finding
Myself thus alter'd with 't.

What's this! Dare not! Do not. You know
and don't dare to tell me? That's the case.
You wouldn't say that you dare not tell yourself,
so it must be that you dare not tell me. Good
Camillo,
the change in your face is like a mirror
which shows that mine has changed too; I must
be involved in this change in some way
as it affects me so much.

CAMILLO
There is a sickness
Which puts some of us in distemper, but
I cannot name the disease; and it is caught
Of you that yet are well.

There is an illness
which makes some of us mad, but
I can't tell you what the disease is; and it is caught
from healthy people like you.

POLIXENES

How! caught of me!	*What! Caught from me!*
Make me not sighted like the basilisk:	*Don't talk as if I kill with a look like a basilisk:*
I have look'd on thousands, who have sped the better	*I have looked at thousands, who have been improved*
By my regard, but kill'd none so. Camillo,--	*through seeing me, but never killed one. Camillo—*
As you are certainly a gentleman, thereto	*as you are certainly a gentleman,*
Clerk-like experienced, which no less adorns	*and also a man of learning, which is just as fitting*
Our gentry than our parents' noble names,	*in a gentleman as the noble ancestry*
In whose success we are gentle,--I beseech you,	*which makes us noble through inheritance–I beg you,*
If you know aught which does behove my knowledge	*if you know anything which you think*
Thereof to be inform'd, imprison't not	*you ought to tell me, don't keep me in the dark.*
In ignorant concealment.	

CAMILLO

I may not answer.	*I can't answer you.*

POLIXENES

A sickness caught of me, and yet I well!	*A sickness caught from me, and yet I'm healthy!*
I must be answer'd. Dost thou hear, Camillo,	*This must be explained. Are you listening, Camillo,*
I conjure thee, by all the parts of man	*I order you, with all the parts of your soul*
Which honour does acknowledge, whereof the least	*which listens to honour, and my request*
Is not this suit of mine, that thou declare	*it is not the least honourable thing, that you tell me*
What incidency thou dost guess of harm	*what threat it is that you think*
Is creeping toward me; how far off, how near;	*is approaching me; how near or far it is;*
Which way to be prevented, if to be;	*how I can stop it, if I can;*
If not, how best to bear it.	*if I can't, how I can cope with it.*

CAMILLO

Sir, I will tell you;	*Sir, I will tell you,*
Since I am charged in honour and by him	*since an appeal has been made to my honour*
That I think honourable: therefore mark my counsel,	*by one whom I think honourable: so, listen to my advice,*
Which must be even as swiftly follow'd as	*which must be followed as soon as I have*
I mean to utter it, or both yourself and me	*said it, otherwise both you and I*
Cry lost, and so good night!	*will be lost, and that will be the end!*

POLIXENES

On, good Camillo.	*Go on, good Camillo.*

CAMILLO

I am appointed him to murder you.	*I have been ordered to murder you.*

POLIXENES

By whom, Camillo?	*By whom, Camillo?*

CAMILLO
By the king.

By the king.

POLIXENES
For what?

Why?

CAMILLO
He thinks, nay, with all confidence he swears,
As he had seen't or been an instrument
To vice you to't, that you have touch'd his queen

Forbiddenly.

He thinks, in fact he is so confident he swears,
as if he had seen it or been the person
he forced you to do it, that you have touched his queen
adulterously.

POLIXENES
O, then my best blood turn
To an infected jelly and my name
Be yoked with his that did betray the Best!
Turn then my freshest reputation to
A savour that may strike the dullest nostril
Where I arrive, and my approach be shunn'd,
Nay, hated too, worse than the great'st infection
That e'er was heard or read!

If that's true by my healthy blood turn
into diseased jelly and may my name
be linked with that of Judas!
May my fragrant reputation be turned
to a stench that disgusts the least sensitive nose
when I appear, and may I be rejected,
no, hated as well, worse than the worst disease
that was ever heard of or read about!

CAMILLO
Swear his thought over
By each particular star in heaven and
By all their influences, you may as well
Forbid the sea for to obey the moon
As or by oath remove or counsel shake
The fabric of his folly, whose foundation

Is piled upon his faith and will continue
The standing of his body.

You can swear that he is wrong
by each individual star in heaven and
by all their properties, you might as well
try and stop the sea obeying the moon
as try through swearing or advice to
destroy the building of his foolishness, whose foundation
rests on his faith, and will last
as long as he lives.

POLIXENES
How should this grow?

How did this come about?

CAMILLO
I know not: but I am sure 'tis safer to
Avoid what's grown than question how 'tis born.

If therefore you dare trust my honesty,
That lies enclosed in this trunk which you
Shall bear along impawn'd, away to-night!

Your followers I will whisper to the business,
And will by twos and threes at several posterns

I do not know: but I do know that it's better
to avoid it now it's happened than to ask what started it.
So, if you dare to trust my honesty,
that is contained within this body which you
shall take along with you as a sign of my good faith, flee tonight!
I will secretly tell your followers what's going on,
and they can sneak out of the city in little groups

27

Clear them o' the city. For myself, I'll put
My fortunes to your service, which are here
By this discovery lost. Be not uncertain;
For, by the honour of my parents, I
Have utter'd truth: which if you seek to prove,
I dare not stand by; nor shall you be safer

Than one condemn'd by the king's own mouth, thereon
His execution sworn.

POLIXENES
I do believe thee:
I saw his heart in 's face. Give me thy hand:
Be pilot to me and thy places shall
Still neighbour mine. My ships are ready and
My people did expect my hence departure
Two days ago. This jealousy
Is for a precious creature: as she's rare,
Must it be great, and as his person's mighty,
Must it be violent, and as he does conceive
He is dishonour'd by a man which ever
Profess'd to him, why, his revenges must
In that be made more bitter. Fear o'ershades me:

Good expedition be my friend, and comfort
The gracious queen, part of his theme, but nothing

Of his ill-ta'en suspicion! Come, Camillo;

I will respect thee as a father if
Thou bear'st my life off hence: let us avoid.

CAMILLO
It is in mine authority to command
The keys of all the posterns: please your highness
To take the urgent hour. Come, sir, away.

Exeunt

*at different gates. As for me, I'll
enter into your service, as by telling you this
I have lost my position here. Don't stop to wonder;
I swear on my parents' honour, I
have told you the truth: if you try to test it,
I do not stay to see it; and you will be in as much danger*

*as one condemned on the king's orders, when
he has sworn to have you executed.*

*I do believe you:
I saw his feelings in his face. Give me your hand:
be my guide and you shall have a position
to match mine. My ships are ready and
my people were expecting me to leave here
two days ago. This jealousy
is for a lovely creature: as she is rare,
it must be great, and as he is great,
it must be violent, and as he believes
he has been dishonoured by a man who always
said he was his friend, why then his revenge
will be made more bitter because of it. Fear hangs over me:*

*may I make a speedy escape, and may
his ill founded suspicions be just as quickly lifted
from his queen
who is such an undeserving victim of them! Come, Camillo,
I will respect you like a father if
you can save my life. Let's escape!*

*I have the authority to command
that the gates be unlocked: your Highness
should move quickly. Come, sir, let's go.*

28

Act 2

Scene 1

SCENE I. A room in LEONTES' palace.

Enter HERMIONE, MAMILLIUS, and Ladies

HERMIONE
Take the boy to you: he so troubles me,
'Tis past enduring.

Take the boy with you: he pesters me so much,
it's intolerable.

First Lady
Come, my gracious lord,
Shall I be your playfellow?

Come on, my gracious lord,
shall I be your playmate?

MAMILLIUS
No, I'll none of you.

No, I want nothing to do with you.

First Lady
Why, my sweet lord?

Why not, my sweet lord?

MAMILLIUS
You'll kiss me hard and speak to me as if
I were a baby still. I love you better.

Because you kiss me roughly and speak to me as if
I was still a baby. I like you better.

Second Lady
And why so, my lord?

And why is that my lord?

MAMILLIUS
Not for because
Your brows are blacker; yet black brows, they say,
Become some women best, so that there be not

Not because
you have blacker eyebrows; although they say
that black eyebrows suit some women best, as long
as there's not

Too much hair there, but in a semicircle
Or a half-moon made with a pen.

too much hair there, just a semicircle
or a half moon drawn on with a pen.

Second Lady
Who taught you this?

Who told you this?

MAMILLIUS
I learnt it out of women's faces. Pray now
What colour are your eyebrows?

I learned it from looking at women. Now tell me,
what colour are your eyebrows?

First Lady
Blue, my lord.

Blue, my lord.

MAMILLIUS

Nay, that's a mock: I have seen a lady's nose
That has been blue, but not her eyebrows.

No, you're joking with me: I have seen a lady
with a blue nose, but not with blue eyebrows.

First Lady
Hark ye;
The queen your mother rounds apace: we shall

You listen to me;
the queen, your mother, has a quickly swelling belly:
we shall

Present our services to a fine new prince
One of these days; and then you'ld wanton with us,
If we would have you.

offer our services to a fine new prince
one of these days; and then you'll want to play with
us, if we would let you.

Second Lady
She is spread of late
Into a goodly bulk: good time encounter her!

She's recently expanded
to a good size: may it all turn out well!

HERMIONE
What wisdom stirs amongst you? Come, sir, now
I am for you again: pray you, sit by us,
And tell 's a tale.

What are you all talking about? Come on, sir, now
I have time for you again: please, sit with me,
and tell me a story.

MAMILLIUS
Merry or sad shall't be?

A happy one or a sad one?

HERMIONE
As merry as you will.

As happy as you like.

MAMILLIUS
A sad tale's best for winter: I have one
Of sprites and goblins.

A sad story's best for winter: I have one
about ghosts and goblins.

HERMIONE
Let's have that, good sir.
Come on, sit down: come on, and do your best
To fright me with your sprites; you're powerful at it.

Let's hear that, good sir.
Come on, sit down: come on, and do your best
to frighten me with your ghosts; you're good at it.

MAMILLIUS
There was a man--

There was a man—

HERMIONE
Nay, come, sit down; then on.

No, come and sit down; then go on.

MAMILLIUS
Dwelt by a churchyard: I will tell it softly;
Yond crickets shall not hear it.

Who lived by a churchyard: I shall whisper it;
it won't disturb those crickets outside.

HERMIONE
Come on, then,
And give't me in mine ear.

Come on, then,
and whisper it to me.

Enter LEONTES, with ANTIGONUS, Lords and others

LEONTES
Was he met there? his train? Camillo with him?

You saw him there? With his entourage? Camillo was with him?

First Lord
Behind the tuft of pines I met them; never
Saw I men scour so on their way: I eyed them
Even to their ships.

I saw them behind the stand of pines; I never saw men in such a hurry: I watched them all the way to their ships.

LEONTES
How blest am I
In my just censure, in my true opinion!
Alack, for lesser knowledge! how accursed
In being so blest! There may be in the cup
A spider steep'd, and one may drink, depart,
And yet partake no venom, for his knowledge
Is not infected: but if one present
The abhorr'd ingredient to his eye, make known
How he hath drunk, he cracks his gorge, his sides,
With violent hefts. I have drunk,
and seen the spider.
Camillo was his help in this, his pander:
There is a plot against my life, my crown;
All's true that is mistrusted: that false villain
Whom I employ'd was pre-employ'd by him:
He has discover'd my design, and I
Remain a pinch'd thing; yea, a very trick
For them to play at will. How came the posterns
So easily open?

How right I was in my judgement, in my sentence! I wish I knew less! How cursed I am in being right! There might be a spider soaked in the cup, and one can drink, leave, and not be poisoned, for his mind is not infected: but if someone shows the horrible ingredient to him, lets him know what he has drunk, he gags and his sides split with violent heaves. I have drunk, and seen the spider. Camillo was his help in this, his pain. There is a plot against my life, and my throne. Everything I suspected is true. That false villain I had in my service was already in his service. He has revealed my plan, and I remain tormented; just something for them to play with. Why was it so easy for them to get through the gates?

First Lord
By his great authority;
Which often hath no less prevail'd than so
On your command.

Because of his position; he often had them opened in the same way at your command.

LEONTES
I know't too well.
Give me the boy: I am glad you did not nurse him:
Though he does bear some signs of me, yet you
Have too much blood in him.

I'm all too aware of that. Give me the boy: I'm glad you didn't breastfeed him: although he does show some elements of me, there is too much of your blood in him.

HERMIONE
What is this? sport?

What's this? A joke?

LEONTES

32

Bear the boy hence; he shall not come about her;
Away with him! and let her sport herself
With that she's big with; for 'tis Polixenes
Has made thee swell thus.

Carry the boy away; he will not be with her;
take him away! Let her play
with the one in her belly; for it is Polixenes
the put that one there.

HERMIONE
But I'd say he had not,
And I'll be sworn you would believe my saying,
Howe'er you lean to the nayward.

But I shall say that he did not,
and I swear that you will believe me,
however much you tried to deny it.

LEONTES
You, my lords,
Look on her, mark her well; be but about
To say 'she is a goodly lady,' and
The justice of your hearts will thereto add
'Tis pity she's not honest, honourable:'
Praise her but for this her without-door form,
Which on my faith deserves high speech, and straight
The shrug, the hum or ha, these petty brands
That calumny doth use--O, I am out--
That mercy does, for calumny will sear

Virtue itself: these shrugs, these hums and ha's,
When you have said 'she's goodly,' come between

Ere you can say 'she's honest:' but be 't known,

From him that has most cause to grieve it should be,
She's an adulteress.

My lords,
take a good look at her; if you're about
to say, 'there's a good lady,' then
the justice in your hearts will add
'it's a pity she's not honest and honourable:'
only praise her for her external appearance,
which I must say certainly does deserve praise,
and eschew the shrugging mumbles falsehood uses-
oh, I'm wrong - I should say that mercy uses,
for falsehood burns mercy itself - the shrugging
mumbles,
when you have said, "she's beautiful," interpose,
before you can say, "she's honest"; but let it be
known,
from the one who has most cause to regret that it's
true:

she's an adulteress.

HERMIONE
Should a villain say so,
The most replenish'd villain in the world,
He were as much more villain: you, my lord,
Do but mistake.

If a villain should say so,
if he was the most complete villain in the world,
he would become even more of a villain: you, my lord,
are making a mistake.

LEONTES
You have mistook, my lady,
Polixenes for Leontes: O thou thing!
Which I'll not call a creature of thy place,

Lest barbarism, making me the precedent,
Should a like language use to all degrees
And mannerly distinguishment leave out
Betwixt the prince and beggar: I have said
She's an adulteress; I have said with whom:
More, she's a traitor and Camillo is
A federary with her, and one that knows

You have made the mistake, my lady,
mistaking Polixenes for Leontes: oh you!
I will not call someone of your rank by the name you
deserve,
in case vulgarity, using me as a precedent,
should use the same sort of language to all ranks
and not make the appropriate distinction between
princes and beggars: I have said
that she's an adulteress; I have said with whom.
What's more, she is a traitor, and Camillo is
her accomplice, someone who knows

What she should shame to know herself
But with her most vile principal, that she's
A bed-swerver, even as bad as those
That vulgars give bold'st titles, ay, and privy
To this their late escape.

the facts which she would be ashamed to have known,
even if only by her foul associate–that she's
a bed hopper, just as bad as the ones
the common people give the worst names; yes,
and she was in on their recent escape.

HERMIONE

No, by my life,
Privy to none of this. How will this grieve you,
When you shall come to clearer knowledge, that
You thus have publish'd me! Gentle my lord,
You scarce can right me throughly then to say
You did mistake.

No, I swear,
I didn't know anything about this. How bad you'll feel,
when you know more about this, that you
have called me these names! My gentle lord,
it will hardly make up for it then to say
that you were mistaken.

LEONTES

No; if I mistake
In those foundations which I build upon,
The centre is not big enough to bear
A school-boy's top. Away with her! to prison!
He who shall speak for her is afar off guilty
But that he speaks.

No, if I'm mistaken
in the foundations I'm building upon,
the Earth is not big enough to support
a schoolboy's top. Take her away! To prison!
Anyone who tries to defend her is guilty
just for speaking.

HERMIONE

There's some ill planet reigns:
I must be patient till the heavens look
With an aspect more favourable. Good my lords,
I am not prone to weeping, as our sex
Commonly are; the want of which vain dew
Perchance shall dry your pities: but I have
That honourable grief lodged here which burns
Worse than tears drown: beseech you all, my lords,
With thoughts so qualified as your charities
Shall best instruct you, measure me; and so

The king's will be perform'd!

Some evil planet is ruling:
I must be patient until the stars
are more in my favour. My good lords,
I do not usually weep, as the rest of my sex
often do; the lack of that pointless moisture
might dry up your pity: but I have
an honourable grief in my heart which burns
worse than any tears: I beg you all, my lords,
soften your thoughts towards me as much
as much as your good instincts tell you, and judge
me;
and so may the king's will be done!

LEONTES

Shall I be heard?

Will my orders be followed?

HERMIONE

Who is't that goes with me? Beseech your highness,

My women may be with me; for you see
My plight requires it. Do not weep, good fools;
There is no cause: when you shall know your
mistress
Has deserved prison, then abound in tears
As I come out: this action I now go on

Who is going to come with me? Please, your
highness,
let my women come with me; you can see
my condition needs them. Don't weep, good fools;
there is no reason to: when you know that your
mistress
deserved to go to prison, then be in floods of tears
when I come out: the thing that I suffer now

Is for my better grace. Adieu, my lord:
I never wish'd to see you sorry; now
I trust I shall. My women, come; you have leave.

will end to my credit. Goodbye, my lord:
I never before wanted to see you apologise; now
I hope that I will. Come on, my women; you have
permission.

LEONTES
Go, do our bidding; hence!

Go on, do as I order; get out!

Exit HERMIONE, guarded; with Ladies

First Lord
Beseech your highness, call the queen again.

Please, your highness, call the queen again.

ANTIGONUS
Be certain what you do, sir, lest your justice
Prove violence; in the which three great ones suffer,

Be certain about what you're doing, sir, in case
your justice proves evil; if it does three great ones
will suffer,

Yourself, your queen, your son.

yourself, your queen, and your son.

First Lord
For her, my lord,
I dare my life lay down and will do't, sir,
Please you to accept it, that the queen is spotless
I' the eyes of heaven and to you; I mean,
In this which you accuse her.

I would lay my life down for her,
my lord, and I will do it;
please accept that the queen is innocent
in the eyes of heaven and your own; I mean,
innocent of what you accuse her.

ANTIGONUS
If it prove
She's otherwise, I'll keep my stables where
I lodge my wife; I'll go in couples with her;
Than when I feel and see her no farther trust her;
For every inch of woman in the world,
Ay, every dram of woman's flesh is false, if she be.

If it's proved
that she is not, I'll turn my wife's lodgings
into a stable; I'll go about with her tethered to me;
I will not trust her to go out of my sight;
for every part of every woman in the world,
every ounce of women's flesh, is false, if she is.

LEONTES
Hold your peaces.

Be quiet.

First Lord
Good my lord,--

My good lord–

ANTIGONUS
It is for you we speak, not for ourselves:
You are abused and by some putter-on
That will be damn'd for't; would I knew the villain,

We are speaking for you, not for ourselves:
you have been tricked by some deceiver
who will be damned for it; I wish I knew who the
villain is,

I would land-damn him. Be she honour-flaw'd,

I would give him a good thrashing. If she is
dishonourable,

I have three daughters; the eldest is eleven

I have three daughters; the oldest is eleven,

35

The second and the third, nine, and some five;
If this prove true, they'll pay for't:
by mine honour,
I'll geld 'em all; fourteen they shall not see,
To bring false generations: they are co-heirs;
And I had rather glib myself than they
Should not produce fair issue.

LEONTES
Cease; no more.
You smell this business with a sense as cold
As is a dead man's nose: but I do see't and feel't
As you feel doing thus; and see withal
The instruments that feel.

ANTIGONUS
If it be so,
We need no grave to bury honesty:
There's not a grain of it the face to sweeten
Of the whole dungy earth.

LEONTES
What! lack I credit?

First Lord
I had rather you did lack than I, my lord,
Upon this ground; and more it would content me
To have her honour true than your suspicion,

Be blamed for't how you might.

LEONTES
Why, what need we
Commune with you of this, but rather follow
Our forceful instigation? Our prerogative
Calls not your counsels, but our natural goodness
Imparts this; which if you, or stupefied
Or seeming so in skill, cannot or will not
Relish a truth like us, inform yourselves
We need no more of your advice: the matter,
The loss, the gain, the ordering on't, is all
Properly ours.

ANTIGONUS
And I wish, my liege,
You had only in your silent judgment tried it,
Without more overture.

the second and third are nine and around five;
if this is true, they'll pay for it:
I swear,
I'd sterilise them all; they would not get to fourteen,
to breed bastards: they are my inheritors;
and I would rather castrate myself than see them
not produce legitimate heirs.

Stop; that's enough.
Your sense of smell in this business is as cold
as a dead man's nose: but I can see it and feel it
as you feel when I this; and I can feel
by touch as well.

If it is true,
we will not need a grave to bury honesty in:
there would not be a grain of it anywhere
to sweeten the dung like face of earth.

What! Do you disbelieve me?

I would rather you were wrong than I, my lord,
in this business; and I would be happier
for her honour to be proved rather than your
suspicion,
however badly that reflected on you.

Why, why should I
debate this with you, when I can carry on
with what I've started? My rights as king
do not require me to ask your advice, I only asked
out of my natural goodness; if you, made stupid
or pretending to have been, cannot or will not
see the truth like I can, then I can tell you
I don't need any more of your advice: this business,
the loss, the gain, and the management of it, is all
rightly down to me.

And I wish, my lord,
you had thought it over yourself first,
without making it public.

LEONTES
How could that be?
Either thou art most ignorant by age,
Or thou wert born a fool. Camillo's flight,
Added to their familiarity,
Which was as gross as ever touch'd conjecture,

That lack'd sight only, nought for approbation

But only seeing, all other circumstances
Made up to the deed, doth push on this proceeding:

Yet, for a greater confirmation,
For in an act of this importance 'twere
Most piteous to be wild, I have dispatch'd in post
To sacred Delphos, to Apollo's temple,
Cleomenes and Dion, whom you know
Of stuff'd sufficiency: now from the oracle

They will bring all; whose spiritual counsel had,

Shall stop or spur me. Have I done well?

First Lord
Well done, my lord.

LEONTES
Though I am satisfied and need no more
Than what I know, yet shall the oracle
Give rest to the minds of others, such as he
Whose ignorant credulity will not
Come up to the truth. So have we thought it good
From our free person she should be confined,
Lest that the treachery of the two fled hence

Be left her to perform. Come, follow us;
We are to speak in public; for this business
Will raise us all.

ANTIGONUS
[Aside]
To laughter, as I take it,
If the good truth were known.
Exeunt

How could I have done that?
Either you've got stupid with age,
or you were born a fool. Camillo's flight,
added to their friendliness,
which was as obvious as anything which ever gave
grounds for suspicion,
only lacking actual visual proof, needing no other
proof
but seeing it, and all the other things
which added up to make it certain the deed had been
done—
make what I'm doing right.
But, for even more confirmation—
for in a matter of such importance it would be
very wrong to act rashly—I have sent messengers
to sacred Delphos, to Apollo's Temple,
Cleomenes and Dion, whom you know
are fully qualified for the task. Now they will bring
back
everything the Oracle says; once I've received that
spiritual counsel
that will either stop me or spur me on. Have I done
right?

You have done well, my lord.

Although I am satisfied and need no more
evidence than what I have, the Oracle shall
put the minds of others at rest, the ones
whose credulous ignorance stops them
from saying the truth. So I thought it best
that she should be locked away from me,
in case the treachery planned by the two who have
fled
should be committed by her. Come, follow me;
I shall speak to the public; for this business
will provoke everybody.

To laughter, I should think,
if the real truth were known.

Scene 2

SCENE II. A prison.

Enter PAULINA, a Gentleman, and Attendants

PAULINA
The keeper of the prison, call to him;
let him have knowledge who I am.

Call the jailer,
Tell him who I am.

Exit Gentleman
Good lady,
No court in Europe is too good for thee;
What dost thou then in prison?

Good lady,
there is no court in Europe that is too good for you;
so what are you doing in prison?

Re-enter Gentleman, with the Gaoler
Now, good sir,
You know me, do you not?

Now, good sir,
you know who I am, don't you?

Gaoler
For a worthy lady
And one whom much I honour.

I know you are a good lady
and one whom I very much respect.

PAULINA
Pray you then,
Conduct me to the queen.

Please, then,
take me to the queen.

Gaoler
I may not, madam:
To the contrary I have express commandment.

I cannot, madam:
I have specific orders not to.

PAULINA
Here's ado,
To lock up honesty and honour from
The access of gentle visitors!
Is't lawful, pray you,
To see her women? any of them? Emilia?

Here's a nice thing,
to lock honesty and honour away from
the access of gentle visitors!
Am I allowed, may I ask,
to see her women? Any of them? Emilia?

Gaoler
So please you, madam,
To put apart these your attendants, I
Shall bring Emilia forth.

If you wouldn't mind, madam,
sending away your attendants, I
will bring Emilia here.

PAULINA
I pray now, call her.
Withdraw yourselves.

Please, call her.
You go outside.

Exeunt Gentleman and Attendants

Gaoler
And, madam,
I must be present at your conference.

And, madam,
I must stay while you talk.

PAULINA
Well, be't so, prithee.

Well, if that's how you want it.

Exit Gaoler
Here's such ado to make no stain a stain

Here is such a business that it turns spotlessness into
a stain

As passes colouring.

that could never be covered up.

Re-enter Gaoler, with EMILIA
Dear gentlewoman,
How fares our gracious lady?

that could never be covered up.
how are things with our gracious lady?

EMILIA
As well as one so great and so forlorn
May hold together: on her frights and griefs,

They are as well as can be expected when one
so great is brought so low: due to her frights and
sorrow,

Which never tender lady hath born greater,

the like of which no gentle lady has ever had to
suffer more,

She is something before her time deliver'd.

she has given birth somewhat ahead of her time.

PAULINA
A boy?

A boy?

EMILIA
A daughter, and a goodly babe,
Lusty and like to live: the queen receives
Much comfort in't; says 'My poor prisoner,
I am innocent as you.'

A daughter, and a good baby,
healthy and likely to survive: the queen takes
much comfort from it; she says, 'my poor prisoner,
I am as innocent as you.'

PAULINA
I dare be sworn
These dangerous unsafe lunes i' the king,
beshrew them!

Curse these dangerous insane notions of the king!

He must be told on't, and he shall: the office
Becomes a woman best; I'll take't upon me:
If I prove honey-mouth'd let my tongue blister
And never to my red-look'd anger be
The trumpet any more. Pray you, Emilia,
Commend my best obedience to the queen:
If she dares trust me with her little babe,
I'll show't the king and undertake to be

He must be told of it, and he shall be: the job
is best done by woman; I'll take it on:
if I talk sweetly to him may my tongue blister
and never be the agent of broadcasting
my anger again. Please, Emilia,
give the Queen my best regards:
if she dares to trust me with her little baby,
I'll show it to the king and promise to be

Her advocate to the loud'st. We do not know
How he may soften at the sight o' the child:
The silence often of pure innocence
Persuades when speaking fails.

her loudest supporter. We do not know
that he may soften when he sees the child:
often the silence of pure innocence
can be persuasive when speech has failed.

EMILIA
Most worthy madam,
Your honour and your goodness is so evident
That your free undertaking cannot miss
A thriving issue: there is no lady living
So meet for this great errand. Please your ladyship
To visit the next room, I'll presently
Acquaint the queen of your most noble offer;
Who but to-day hammer'd of this design,
But durst not tempt a minister of honour,
Lest she should be denied.

Most worthy madam,
your honour and your goodness is so obvious
that this task you undertake cannot help but
achieve success: there is no lady alive
so suitable for this great mission. If your ladyship
would please go into the next room, I'll shortly
tell the queen about your most noble offer;
just today she was talking of something like this,
but didn't dare to put it to the test,
in case she should fail.

PAULINA
Tell her, Emilia.
I'll use that tongue I have: if wit flow from't

As boldness from my bosom, let 't not be doubted
I shall do good.

Tell her, Emilia.
I'll use my skill in speaking: if the wisdom of my tongue
matches the courage in my heart, do not doubt
that I will do good.

EMILIA
Now be you blest for it!
I'll to the queen: please you,
come something nearer.

May God bless you for it!
I'll go to the queen: please,
come a little closer.

Gaoler
Madam, if't please the queen to send the babe,
I know not what I shall incur to pass it,
Having no warrant.

Madam, if the queen wants to send the baby,
I don't know what will happen to me for letting it go,
as I have no permission to do so.

PAULINA
You need not fear it, sir:
This child was prisoner to the womb and is
By law and process of great nature thence
Freed and enfranchised, not a party to
The anger of the king nor guilty of,
If any be, the trespass of the queen.

You need not worry, sir:
this child was a prisoner in the womb and has been
by law and the great processes of nature freed
from there; she was not the subject of
the king's anger, nor guilty of,
if there is any guilt, any wrongdoing by the queen.

Gaoler
I do believe it.

I believe that.

PAULINA

Do not you fear: upon mine honour,
I will stand betwixt you and danger.
Exeunt

Don't be afraid: I promise you,
I will intervene between you and danger.

Scene 3

SCENE III. A room in LEONTES' palace.

Enter LEONTES, ANTIGONUS, Lords, and Servants

LEONTES
Nor night nor day no rest: it is but weakness
To bear the matter thus; mere weakness. If
The cause were not in being,--part o' the cause,

She the adulteress; for the harlot king
Is quite beyond mine arm, out of the blank
And level of my brain, plot-proof; but she
I can hook to me: say that she were gone,
Given to the fire, a moiety of my rest
Might come to me again. Who's there?

I can't sleep, night or day: it's just weakness
to let it affect me like this; just weakness. If
the reason was no longer in existence–part of the
reason,
she is the adulteress; the fornicating king
is quite out of my reach, out of the range
of my shots, plot–proof; but I can
deal with her: what if she were gone,
burned alive, maybe a portion of my rest
might come back to me. Who's there?

First Servant
My lord?

My lord?

LEONTES
How does the boy?

How is the boy?

First Servant
He took good rest to-night;
'Tis hoped his sickness is discharged.

He had a good sleep tonight;
we hope that the illness is passed.

LEONTES
To see his nobleness!
Conceiving the dishonour of his mother,
He straight declined, droop'd, took it deeply,

Fasten'd and fix'd the shame on't in himself,
Threw off his spirit, his appetite, his sleep,

And downright languish'd. Leave me solely: go,
See how he fares.

See how noble he is!
Seeing the shame of his mother,
he fell straight into a decline, drooped, took it very
hard,
assumed all the guilt of it for himself,
became low spirited, lost his appetite, could not
sleep,
and completely weakened. Leave me alone.
Go and see how he is.

Exit Servant

Fie, fie! no thought of him:
The thought of my revenges that way
Recoil upon me: in himself too mighty,
And in his parties, his alliance; let him be
Until a time may serve: for present vengeance,
Take it on her. Camillo and Polixenes
Laugh at me, make their pastime at my sorrow:
They should not laugh if I could reach them, nor
Shall she within my power.

Enter PAULINA, with a child

First Lord
You must not enter.

PAULINA
Nay, rather, good my lords, be second to me:
Fear you his tyrannous passion more, alas,
Than the queen's life? a gracious innocent soul,

More free than he is jealous.

ANTIGONUS
That's enough.

Second Servant
Madam, he hath not slept tonight; commanded
None should come at him.

PAULINA
Not so hot, good sir:
I come to bring him sleep. 'Tis such as you,
That creep like shadows by him and do sigh
At each his needless heavings, such as you
Nourish the cause of his awaking: I
Do come with words as medicinal as true,

Honest as either, to purge him of that humour

That presses him from sleep.

LEONTES
What noise there, ho?

PAULINA
No noise, my lord; but needful conference
About some gossips for your highness.

Come on now, don't think about him!
The very thought of taking my revenge in that way
is ridiculous: he is too mighty on his own,
and he has allies. Let him be
until the time is right; for the moment take revenge
on her. Camillo and Polixenes
laugh at me, my sorrow is their entertainment.
They would not laugh if I could get at them, and
as she is within my power she shall not laugh.

You can't come in.

No, my good lords, support me:
alas, are you too afraid to face his tyrannous anger
when the queen's life is at stake? She is a gracious
innocent
who is as guiltless as he is jealous.

That's enough.

Madam, he has not slept tonight; he ordered
that nobody should disturb him.

Don't be so hasty, good sir:
I have come to help him sleep. It's people like you,
that tiptoe around him and pity
all his needless commotion, your type
is feeding the thing which keeps him awake: I
have come with words which are as good for him as
they are true,
as honest as you could wish for, to drive out the
mood
that keeps him from his sleep.

What's the racket out there?

No racket, my lord; just a necessary discussion
about some godparents for your highness.

LEONTES
How!
Away with that audacious lady! Antigonus,
I charged thee that she should not come about me:
I knew she would.

What!
Take that cheeky lady away! Antigonus,
I ordered you that she should not come near me:
I knew she would try.

ANTIGONUS
I told her so, my lord,
On your displeasure's peril and on mine,
She should not visit you.

I told her so, my lord,
I told her that she should not visit you
or she would face your anger and mine.

LEONTES
What, canst not rule her?

What, can't you control her?

PAULINA
From all dishonesty he can: in this,
Unless he take the course that you have done,
Commit me for committing honour, trust it,

He shall not rule me.

He can stop me from doing anything dishonourable:
in this matter, unless he follows your course,
and imprisons me for being honourable, I can assure you
that he will not tell me what to do.

ANTIGONUS
La you now, you hear:
When she will take the rein I let her run;
But she'll not stumble.

There, you see how she talks:
when I can control her I let her have her head;
but she won't slip.

PAULINA
Good my liege, I come;
And, I beseech you, hear me, who profess
Myself your loyal servant, your physician,
Your most obedient counsellor, yet that dare
Less appear so in comforting your evils,

Than such as most seem yours: I say, I come

From your good queen.

My good lord, I am coming;
and, I beg you, listen to me, who declares
that I am your loyal servant, your doctor,
your most obedient counsellor, but I dare
to appear differently by not supporting your wrongdoing,
which is more than most of your people will do: I tell you, I have come
from your good queen.

LEONTES
Good queen!

Good queen!

PAULINA
Good queen, my lord,
Good queen; I say good queen;
And would by combat make her good, so were I
A man, the worst about you.

Good queen, my lord,
good queen; I say good queen;
I would prove her goodness in combat, if I were
a man, even if I were the weakest of you all.

LEONTES

Force her hence.

Throw her out.

PAULINA

Let him that makes but trifles of his eyes
First hand me: on mine own accord I'll off;

But first I'll do my errand. The good queen,
For she is good, hath brought you forth a daughter;
Here 'tis; commends it to your blessing.

If anyone doesn't care about his eyes,
let him lay hands on me: I'll leave of my own
accord;
but first I'll do my errand. The good queen,
for she is good, has produced a daughter for use;
here it is; she asks you to bless it.

Laying down the child

LEONTES

Out!
A mankind witch! Hence with her, out o' door:
A most intelligencing bawd!

Get out!
A mannish witch! Throw her out, out the door:
a scheming slut!

PAULINA

Not so:
I am as ignorant in that as you
In so entitling me, and no less honest
Than you are mad; which is enough, I'll warrant,
As this world goes, to pass for honest.

I am not:
I am as ignorant of that as you are
by calling me it, and I am as honourable
as you are mad; which I think is enough,
in the eyes of the world, to be seen as honourable.

LEONTES

Traitors!
Will you not push her out? Give her the bastard.
Thou dotard! thou art woman-tired, unroosted

By thy dame Partlet here. Take up the bastard;
Take't up, I say; give't to thy crone.

Traitors!
Will you not throw her out? Give her the bastard.
You old fool! You are henpecked, pushed off your
perch
by this old hen. Pick up the bastard;
pick it up, I say; give it to your bleating wife.

PAULINA

For ever
Unvenerable be thy hands, if thou
Takest up the princess by that forced baseness
Which he has put upon't!

Your hands will be for ever
despised, if you
pick up the princess under that foul name
which he has given her!

LEONTES

He dreads his wife.

He's afraid of his wife.

PAULINA

So I would you did; then 'twere past all doubt
You'ld call your children yours.

I wish you were; then you would definitely
acknowledge your children as your own.

LEONTES

44

Original	Modern
A nest of traitors!	*A nest of traitors!*
ANTIGONUS	
I am none, by this good light.	*I am not one, I swear.*
PAULINA	
Nor I, nor any	*Nor am I, nor is anyone here*
But one that's here, and that's himself, for he	*but one, and that's him, for he*
The sacred honour of himself, his queen's,	*has slandered, in terms sharper than a sword's sting,*
His hopeful son's, his babe's, betrays to slander,	*the sacred honour of himself, his queen,*
Whose sting is sharper than the sword's;	*his son and heir, and his baby, and he will not—*
and will not--	
For, as the case now stands, it is a curse	*for as matters stand unfortunately*
He cannot be compell'd to't--once remove	*he cannot be forced to do it—get rid of*
The root of his opinion, which is rotten	*his wrong ideas, which are as rotten*
As ever oak or stone was sound.	*as oak and stone are sound.*
LEONTES	
A callat	*A harridan*
Of boundless tongue, who late hath beat her husband	*of endless words, who has just beaten her husband*
And now baits me! This brat is none of mine;	*and now attacks me! This brat is nothing to do with me;*
It is the issue of Polixenes:	*Polixenes is its father:*
Hence with it, and together with the dam	*take it away, and throw it into the fire*
Commit them to the fire!	*alongside its mother!*
PAULINA	
It is yours;	*It is yours,*
And, might we lay the old proverb to your charge,	*and, we might quote the old proverb to you,*
So like you, 'tis the worse. Behold, my lords,	*unluckily for it it is very like you. Look, my lords,*
Although the print be little, the whole matter	*although the picture is small, the whole substance*
And copy of the father, eye, nose, lip,	*and image of the father, eye, nose, lips,*
The trick of's frown, his forehead, nay, the valley,	*the same look in the frown, the forehead, the wrinkles,*
The pretty dimples of his chin and cheek,	*the pretty dimples of the chin and cheek,*
His smiles,	*his smiles,*
The very mould and frame of hand, nail, finger:	*the exact cast and shape of hand, nails and fingers:*
And thou, good goddess Nature, which hast made it	*and you, good Goddess nature, have made it*
So like to him that got it, if thou hast	*so like its father, if you also*
The ordering of the mind too, 'mongst all colours	*arranged its mind, don't allow*
No yellow in't, lest she suspect, as he does,	*any jealousy in there, in case she suspects, as he does,*
Her children not her husband's!	*that her children are not her husband's.*
LEONTES	
A gross hag	*A gross hag*
And, lozel, thou art worthy to be hang'd,	*and you, worthless lout, you should be hanged*
That wilt not stay her tongue.	*for not keeping her quiet.*

ANTIGONUS
Hang all the husbands
That cannot do that feat, you'll leave yourself
Hardly one subject.

Hang all the husbands
that can't manage that, and you'll have
hardly anyone left in the country.

LEONTES
Once more, take her hence.

I say again, take her away.

PAULINA
A most unworthy and unnatural lord
Can do no more.

This is a most unworthy and unnatural king;
we can do no more.

LEONTES
I'll ha' thee burnt.

I'll have you burnt.

PAULINA
I care not:
It is an heretic that makes the fire,
Not she which burns in't. I'll not call you tyrant;

But this most cruel usage of your queen,
Not able to produce more accusation
Than your own weak-hinged fancy, something savours
Of tyranny and will ignoble make you,
Yea, scandalous to the world.

I don't care:
it would be a heretic that lit the fire,
she who burnt in it would be none. I won't call you a tyrant;
but this terrible cruel treatment of your queen,
based on no more evidence
than your own weak minded imagination, does look
like tyranny and will make you dishonourable,
and the world will be scandalised.

LEONTES
On your allegiance,
Out of the chamber with her! Were I a tyrant,
Where were her life? she durst not call me so,
If she did know me one. Away with her!

By the oath you have sworn,
throw her out of the room! If I were a tyrant,
would she still be alive? If she knew I was one,
she would not dare to call me one. Throw her out!

PAULINA
I pray you, do not push me; I'll be gone.
Look to your babe, my lord; 'tis yours:
Jove send her
A better guiding spirit! What needs these hands?
You, that are thus so tender o'er his follies,
Will never do him good, not one of you.
So, so: farewell; we are gone.

Please, do not push me; I'll go.
Look at your baby, my lord; it is yours:
may Jove give her
a better guide than you! What use are these people?
All of you, who play along with his madness,
will never do him any good, not one of you.
There it is: farewell; we are going.

Exit

LEONTES
Thou, traitor, hast set on thy wife to this.

You, traitor, egged your wife on to do this.

My child? away with't! Even thou, that hast
A heart so tender o'er it, take it hence
And see it instantly consumed with fire;
Even thou and none but thou. Take it up straight:

Within this hour bring me word 'tis done,
And by good testimony, or I'll seize thy life,
With what thou else call'st thine. If thou refuse
And wilt encounter with my wrath, say so;
The bastard brains with these my proper hands
Shall I dash out. Go, take it to the fire;
For thou set'st on thy wife.

ANTIGONUS
I did not, sir:
These lords, my noble fellows, if they please,
Can clear me in't.

Lords
We can: my royal liege,
He is not guilty of her coming hither.

LEONTES
You're liars all.

First Lord
Beseech your highness, give us better credit:
We have always truly served you, and beseech you

So to esteem of us, and on our knees we beg,
As recompense of our dear services
Past and to come, that you do change this purpose,

Which being so horrible, so bloody, must
Lead on to some foul issue: we all kneel.

LEONTES
I am a feather for each wind that blows:
Shall I live on to see this bastard kneel
And call me father? better burn it now
Than curse it then. But be it; let it live.
It shall not neither. You, sir, come you hither;
You that have been so tenderly officious
With Lady Margery, your midwife there,
To save this bastard's life,--for 'tis a bastard,
So sure as this beard's grey,
--what will you adventure
To save this brat's life?

My child? A curse on it! I order you, who
cares for it so much, to take it out
and have it burnt at once;
I order you and nobody else to do this. Pick it up at
once:
within the hour bring me word that is is done,
and with good evidence, or I shall take your life
and everything else belonging to you. If you refuse
and want to take on my anger, say so;
I shall bash out these bastard brains
with my own good hands. Go on, take it to the fire;
because it was you who encouraged your wife.

I did not, sir:
these lords, my noble peers, if they wish,
can clear me of it.

We can: my royal lord,
he is innocent of her coming here.

You're all liars.

I beg your highness, give us more credit than that:
we have always served you faithfully, and we beg
you
here on our knees to do us the honour,
in return for the kind services
we have done and will do you, that you change your
mind,
which is so horrible and bloody that it must
come to a terrible end: we all kneel to you.

I am a plaything for the fates:
should I live on to see this bastard kneel
and call me father? It's better to burn it now
than to curse it then. But so be it; let it live.
It shan't do that. You, sir, come here;
you have been so softhearted,
with that gabbling woman there,
to save this bastard's life–for it is a bastard,
as certainly as this beard is grey–
what will you risk
to say this brat's life?

ANTIGONUS
Any thing, my lord,
That my ability may undergo
And nobleness impose: at least thus much:
I'll pawn the little blood which I have left
To save the innocent: any thing possible.

LEONTES
It shall be possible. Swear by this sword
Thou wilt perform my bidding.

ANTIGONUS
I will, my lord.

LEONTES
Mark and perform it, see'st thou! for the fail
Of any point in't shall not only be
Death to thyself but to thy lewd-tongued wife,
Whom for this time we pardon. We enjoin thee,
As thou art liege-man to us, that thou carry
This female bastard hence and that thou bear it
To some remote and desert place quite out
Of our dominions, and that there thou leave it,
Without more mercy, to its own protection
And favour of the climate. As by strange fortune
It came to us, I do in justice charge thee,
On thy soul's peril and thy body's torture,

That thou commend it strangely to some place
Where chance may nurse or end it. Take it up.

ANTIGONUS
I swear to do this, though a present death
Had been more merciful. Come on, poor babe:
Some powerful spirit instruct the kites and ravens
To be thy nurses! Wolves and bears, they say
Casting their savageness aside have done
Like offices of pity. Sir, be prosperous
In more than this deed does require! And blessing
Against this cruelty fight on thy side,
Poor thing, condemn'd to loss!

Exit with the child

LEONTES
No, I'll not rear
Another's issue.

Anything, my lord,
that I have the ability to do
and that is honourable: I'll do at least this:
I'll risk the life I have left
to save the child: I'll do anything.

This shall happen. Swear on this sword
that you will do as I say.

I will, my lord.

Listen and make sure you do it! If you
miss out any point of it it won't only mean
death to you but for your foulmouthed wife,
whom I pardon for now. I order you,
as you are sworn to obedience to me, that you take
this female bastard away and carry it
to some remote and deserted place outside
my kingdom; you must leave it there,
without doing anything more for it,
to fend for itself. Since it came here
via a foreigner, it's only justice that I order you,
to save you from damnation for your soul and
torture for your body,
to leave it in some foreign place
where fate may nurture it or kill it.

I swear I'll do this, though an instant death
would be more merciful. Come on, poor baby:
may some powerful spirit order the kites and ravens
to take care of you! They say that wolves and bears
have put aside their savagery to do
similar acts of care. Sir, may you have more luck
than you deserve for doing this deed! And may you
find mercy that outweighs this cruelty,
Poor baby, condemned to destruction!

No, I will not raise
someone else's child.

Enter a Servant

Servant
Please your highness, posts
From those you sent to the oracle are come
An hour since: Cleomenes and Dion,
Being well arrived from Delphos, are both landed,

Hasting to the court.

Your Highness, messages
have come an hour ago from the ones you sent
to the Oracle: Cleomenes and Dion,
having made a good journey from Delphos, have
both landed,
and are hurrying to the court.

First Lord
So please you, sir, their speed
Hath been beyond account.

Well, sir, that's an amazingly
quick journey.

LEONTES
Twenty-three days
They have been absent: 'tis good speed; foretells
The great Apollo suddenly will have
The truth of this appear. Prepare you, lords;
Summon a session, that we may arraign
Our most disloyal lady, for, as she hath
Been publicly accused, so shall she have
A just and open trial. While she lives
My heart will be a burthen to me. Leave me,
And think upon my bidding.

They have been gone
twenty-three days: they've made good time; it shows
that great Apollo wants the truth of this to appear
quickly. Make preparations, lords;
call the court together, so we can charge
my disloyal wife, for, as she has
been publicly accused, she shall also have
a fair and open trial. My heart will always be heavy
as long as she is alive. Leave me,
and get on with my orders.

Exeunt

Act 3

Scene 1

SCENE I. A sea-port in Sicilia.

Enter CLEOMENES and DION

CLEOMENES
The climate's delicate, the air most sweet,
Fertile the isle, the temple much surpassing
The common praise it bears.

The climate is moderate, the air is beautiful,
the island is fertile, and the temple is even greater
than the praise one hears of it.

DION
I shall report,
For most it caught me, the celestial habits,

Methinks I so should term them, and the reverence

Of the grave wearers. O, the sacrifice!
How ceremonious, solemn and unearthly
It was i' the offering!

I shall report
that the thing which most caught my eye was the
heavenly clothes,
which is what I think is I should call them, and the
holiness
of the grave ones who wore them. Oh, the sacrifice!
Have dignified, solemn and unearthly
the offering was.

CLEOMENES
But of all, the burst
And the ear-deafening voice o' the oracle,
Kin to Jove's thunder, so surprised my sense,
That I was nothing.

But out of everything, the eruption
of the deafening voice of the Oracle,
seeming like Jove's thunder, astonished me,
so I felt like nothing.

DION
If the event o' the journey
Prove as successful to the queen,--O be't so!--
As it hath been to us rare, pleasant, speedy,
The time is worth the use on't.

If the outcome of the journey
it is as successful for the queen–please let it be so!–
As it has been for us, exciting, pleasant and quick,
then the time has been well spent.

CLEOMENES
Great Apollo
Turn all to the best! These proclamations,
So forcing faults upon Hermione,
I little like.

May great Apollo
make everything turn out for the best!
I don't like these proclamations
which attribute all these faults to Hermione.

DION
The violent carriage of it
Will clear or end the business: when the oracle,
Thus by Apollo's great divine seal'd up,
Shall the contents discover, something rare
Even then will rush to knowledge. Go: fresh horses!

And gracious be the issue!

The rushed way it is being dealt with
will either throw out or finish the business: when
the contents of this prediction are revealed,
which was sealed up by Apollo's great priest,
something amazing will come to light. Let's go:
bring fresh horses!
And may things turn out well!

Exeunt

Scene 2

SCENE II. A court of Justice.

Enter LEONTES, Lords, and Officers

LEONTES
This sessions, to our great grief we pronounce,
Even pushes 'gainst our heart: the party tried
The daughter of a king, our wife, and one
Of us too much beloved. Let us be clear'd
Of being tyrannous, since we so openly
Proceed in justice, which shall have due course,
Even to the guilt or the purgation.
Produce the prisoner.

I announce this trial with great sadness,
it pulls at my heartstrings: the person being tried
is the daughter of a king , my wife, someone
I loved too much. Do not let me be accused
of being a tyrant, since we are holding
an open trial, which will follow due procedures,
whether it produces a guilty verdict or an acquittal.
Bring out the prisoner.

Officer
It is his highness' pleasure that the queen
Appear in person here in court. Silence!

It is his Highness' order that the queen
should appear in person here in court. Silence!

Enter HERMIONE guarded; PAULINA and Ladies attending

LEONTES
Read the indictment.

Read the indictment.

Officer
[Reads] Hermione, queen to the worthy
Leontes, king of Sicilia, thou art here accused and
arraigned of high treason, in committing adultery
with Polixenes, king of Bohemia, and conspiring
with Camillo to take away the life of our sovereign
lord the king, thy royal husband: the pretence
whereof being by circumstances partly laid open,
thou, Hermione, contrary to the faith and allegiance
of a true subject, didst counsel and aid them, for
their better safety, to fly away by night.

Hermione, queen of the worthy
Leontes, king of Sicily, you are hereby accused and
charged with high treason, by committing adultery
with Polixenes, king of Bohemia, and conspiring
with Camillo to murder our royal
lord the king, your royal husband: as the plan
was partly discovered,
you, Hermione, going against the faith and loyalty
of the true subject, did advise and help them, for
their own safety, to flee in the night.

HERMIONE
Since what I am to say must be but that
Which contradicts my accusation and
The testimony on my part no other
But what comes from myself, it shall scarce boot me
To say 'not guilty:' mine integrity
Being counted falsehood, shall, as I express it,
Be so received. But thus: if powers divine
Behold our human actions, as they do,
I doubt not then but innocence shall make

Since what I have to say has to be
a rebuttal of this accusation, and
as the only testimony in my favour
is what comes from me, it won't help me
to say 'not guilty ': my integrity
being doubted, it will be seen as false
when I say it. But I do say, if the heavenly powers
observe our human actions (as they do),
I have no doubts that innocence will put

False accusation blush and tyranny
Tremble at patience. You, my lord, best know,

Who least will seem to do so, my past life

Hath been as continent, as chaste, as true,
As I am now unhappy; which is more
Than history can pattern, though devised
And play'd to take spectators. For behold me

A fellow of the royal bed, which owe
A moiety of the throne a great king's daughter,
The mother to a hopeful prince, here standing
To prate and talk for life and honour 'fore

Who please to come and hear. For life, I prize it

As I weigh grief, which I would spare: for honour,

'Tis a derivative from me to mine,
And only that I stand for. I appeal
To your own conscience, sir, before Polixenes
Came to your court, how I was in your grace,

How merited to be so; since he came,
With what encounter so uncurrent I
Have strain'd to appear thus: if one jot beyond

The bound of honour, or in act or will

That way inclining, harden'd be the hearts

Of all that hear me, and my near'st of kin
Cry fie upon my grave!

LEONTES
I ne'er heard yet
That any of these bolder vices wanted
Less impudence to gainsay what they did
Than to perform it first.

HERMIONE
That's true enough;
Through 'tis a saying, sir, not due to me.

LEONTES
You will not own it.

false accusations to shame, and tyranny
will shake in the face of steadfastness. You, my lord,
know best
(even this at the moment you seem to know least)
that my past life
has been as moderate, as chaste, as loyal
as I am now unhappy; and that is more
than a story can tell, even if it was
written and played out for spectators. For look at
me,
who had a share of the royal bed, who owns
a share of the throne, a great king's daughter,
the mother of an inheriting prince, standing here
to uselessly talk to try and save my life and honour
in front of
anyone who cares to come and listen. As for life, I
value it
as I value grief (which I could well do without): but
honour
is something that my children will inherit from me,
and that's the only thing I'm fighting for. I appeal
to your own conscience, Sir; before Polixenes
came to your court, remember how much you loved
me,
and how much I deserved it; since he came,
what behaviour so out of the ordinary and so
wrong have I committed to put me in this position: if
I've gone
a single inch over the boundaries of honour, or have
looked
as if I was going that way in thought or deed, may
all the hearts that
hear me be hardened, and may my closest family
disrespect my grave!

Everyone knows
that the worst sinners have just as much
cheek in denying what they have done
as they had to do it in the first place.

That's true enough;
though it is saying, sir, that you can't apply to me.

You won't admit to it.

54

HERMIONE

More than mistress of
Which comes to me in name of fault, I must not
At all acknowledge. For Polixenes,
With whom I am accused, I do confess
I loved him as in honour he required,
With such a kind of love as might become
A lady like me, with a love even such,
So and no other, as yourself commanded:
Which not to have done I think had been in me
Both disobedience and ingratitude
To you and toward your friend, whose love had spoke,
Even since it could speak, from an infant, freely
That it was yours. Now, for conspiracy,
I know not how it tastes; though it be dish'd
For me to try how: all I know of it

Is that Camillo was an honest man;
And why he left your court, the gods themselves,

Wotting no more than I, are ignorant.

*I won't admit to anything
except for that which I am now being accused of
being at fault in. With reference to Polixenes,
my fellow accused, I admit
that I loved him as his position demanded,
with the kind of love which is suitable for
a lady like me; with the kind of love, indeed,
and no other, that you ordered me to show:
if I had not done so I think I would have been
both disobedient and ungrateful
to you, and towards your friend, who had,
from a child, ever since he could speak, freely
offered you his love. Now, as for conspiracy,
I don't know what it's like, in fact I
wouldn't be able to recognise it in front of me: all I
know about it,
is that Camillo was an honest man;
and as to why he left your court, the gods
themselves
(if they know no more than I do) do not know.*

LEONTES

You knew of his departure, as you know
What you have underta'en to do in's absence.

*You knew about his departure, as you know
what you have promised to do while he is away.*

HERMIONE

Sir,
You speak a language that I understand not:
My life stands in the level of your dreams,
Which I'll lay down.

*Sir,
you are speaking a language I can't understand:
my life is at the mercy of your delusions,
and I'll lay it down.*

LEONTES

Your actions are my dreams;

You had a bastard by Polixenes,
And I but dream'd it! As you were past all shame,--

Those of your fact are so--so past all truth:

Which to deny concerns more than avails; for as

Thy brat hath been cast out, like to itself,
No father owning it,--which is, indeed,
More criminal in thee than it,--so thou
Shalt feel our justice, in whose easiest passage
Look for no less than death.

*What you call my delusions are things you have
done;
you had a bastard with Polixenes,
and you call it a delusion! As you are beyond all
shame—
criminals like you always are—so you are beyond all
truth:
by denying it you're only making it worse for
yourself;
just as your brat has been thrown out, left to itself,
with no father claiming it—which is, of course,
more your fault than its—so you
will feel my justice, and the lightest sentence
you can hope for is death.*

HERMIONE

Sir, spare your threats:
The bug which you would fright me with I seek.

To me can life be no commodity:
The crown and comfort of my life, your favour,
I do give lost; for I do feel it gone,
But know not how it went. My second joy
And first-fruits of my body, from his presence
I am barr'd, like one infectious. My third comfort

Starr'd most unluckily, is from my breast,

The innocent milk in its most innocent mouth,

Haled out to murder: myself on every post
Proclaimed a strumpet: with immodest hatred
The child-bed privilege denied, which 'longs

To women of all fashion; lastly, hurried

Here to this place, i' the open air, before
I have got strength of limit. Now, my liege,
Tell me what blessings I have here alive,
That I should fear to die? Therefore proceed.
But yet hear this: mistake me not; no life,
I prize it not a straw, but for mine honour,
Which I would free, if I shall be condemn'd
Upon surmises, all proofs sleeping else
But what your jealousies awake, I tell you
'Tis rigor and not law. Your honours all,
I do refer me to the oracle:
Apollo be my judge!

First Lord

This your request
Is altogether just: therefore bring forth,
And in Apollos name, his oracle.

Exeunt certain Officers

HERMIONE

The Emperor of Russia was my father:
O that he were alive, and here beholding
His daughter's trial! that he did but see
The flatness of my misery, yet with eyes
Of pity, not revenge!

Sir, save your threats:
the terror you are trying to frighten me with, I wish for.
To me life is now useless;
the pride and joy of my life, your love,
I have given up as lost, for I can feel it has gone,
though I do not know why it went. My second joy
is my firstborn, and I am banned from his presence
like someone with an infectious disease. My third comfort
(born under an unlucky star) has been torn from my breast
(with the innocent milk still in its most innocent mouth)
and thrown out to die; I am declared
a whore on every side, excessive hatred
has taken from me the privilege of the maternity bed, which belongs
to all women of every rank; lastly I have been hurried here,
to this place, exposed to the cold, before
I have got my strength back. Now, my lord,
tell me what blessings there are in my life
that should make me afraid to die? So carry on.
But hear this: do not mistake me: I don't
care a jot for life, but I want to preserve
my honour: if I'm going to be condemned
by guesses, with no other evidence
except what your jealousy has made up,
I tell you that this is not a fair process. All you lords,
I put my case to the Oracle:
may Apollo be my judge!

This request of yours
is completely fair: so bring out,
in the name of Apollo, his oracle.

The Emperor of Russia was my father:
I wish that he were alive and here to see
his daughter's trial! If he could only see
my overwhelming misery, but with eyes
of pity, not revenge!

Re-enter Officers, with CLEOMENES and DION

Officer
You here shall swear upon this sword of justice,
That you, Cleomenes and Dion, have
Been both at Delphos, and from thence have brought
The seal'd-up oracle, by the hand deliver'd
Of great Apollo's priest; and that, since then,
You have not dared to break the holy seal
Nor read the secrets in't.

You shall now swear upon this sword of justice
that you, Cleomenes and Dion, have
both been to Delphos, and have brought from there
a sealed oracle, delivered by the hand
of great Apollo's priest; and that, since then,
you have not dared to break the holy seal,
nor read the secrets inside.

CLEOMENES DION
All this we swear.

We swear to this.

LEONTES
Break up the seals and read.

Break open the seals and read it.

Officer
[Reads] Hermione is chaste;
Polixenes blameless; Camillo a true subject;
Leontes
a jealous tyrant; his innocent babe truly begotten;
and the king shall live without an heir, if that
which is lost be not found.

Hermione is chaste;
Polixenes blameless; Camillo a faithful subject;
Leontes
is a jealous tyrant; he is innocent baby is legitimate;
and the king will live without an heir, if what
has been lost is not recovered.

Lords
Now blessed be the great Apollo!

Blessings on the great Apollo!

HERMIONE
Praised!

Praise him!

LEONTES
Hast thou read truth?

Have you read this truly?

Officer
Ay, my lord; even so
As it is here set down.

Yes, my lord; exactly
as it is written down here.

LEONTES
There is no truth at all i' the oracle:
The sessions shall proceed: this is mere falsehood.

There is no truth at all in this oracle:
the trial shall proceed: these are just lies.

Enter Servant

Servant
My lord the king, the king!

My lord the king, the king!

57

LEONTES
What is the business?

What's the matter?

Servant
O sir, I shall be hated to report it!
The prince your son, with mere conceit and fear

Of the queen's speed, is gone.

Oh Sir, you will hate me for saying it!
Your son the prince, seeing his mother dishonoured and fearing
her fate, has gone.

LEONTES
How! gone!

What! Gone!

Servant
Is dead.

He's dead.

LEONTES
Apollo's angry; and the heavens themselves
Do strike at my injustice.

Apollo's angry; and the heavens themselves
are punishing my injustice.

HERMIONE swoons
How now there!

What's going on there!

PAULINA
This news is mortal to the queen: look down
And see what death is doing.

This news is fatal to the queen: look down
and see how death has struck her.

LEONTES
Take her hence:
Her heart is but o'ercharged; she will recover:
I have too much believed mine own suspicion:
Beseech you, tenderly apply to her
Some remedies for life.

Take her away:
she is just overcome: she will recover.
I have believed my own suspicions too much:
please, gently give her
some treatment to recover her.

Exeunt PAULINA and Ladies, with HERMIONE
Apollo, pardon
My great profaneness 'gainst thine oracle!
I'll reconcile me to Polixenes,
New woo my queen, recall the good Camillo,
Whom I proclaim a man of truth, of mercy;
For, being transported by my jealousies
To bloody thoughts and to revenge, I chose
Camillo for the minister to poison
My friend Polixenes: which had been done,
But that the good mind of Camillo tardied

My swift command, though I with death and with

Apollo, forgive
my great blasphemy against your Oracle!
I'll make things up with Polixenes,
win my queen back, recall the good Camillo,
whom I declare to be a man of truth and mercy:
for being transported by my jealousy
to bloody thoughts and revenge, I chose
Camillo to give poison
to my friend Polixenes: this would have happened,
except for the fact that the good mind of Camillo delayed
my orders that it should be done at once; even though I threatened

Reward did threaten and encourage him,

Not doing 't and being done: he, most humane

And fill'd with honour, to my kingly guest
Unclasp'd my practise, quit his fortunes here,
Which you knew great, and to the hazard
Of all encertainties himself commended,
No richer than his honour: how he glisters
Thorough my rust! and how his pity
Does my deeds make the blacker!

and encouraged him with death and reward respectively,
according to whether he did it or not. He (most humane
and honourable) told my royal guest
what I was planning, left all his fortune here
(which you know was great) and gave himself up
to great uncertainty rather than lose his honour,
which was all he had now: how he shines
through my rust! How his goodness
makes my behaviour look blacker!

Re-enter PAULINA

PAULINA
Woe the while!
O, cut my lace, lest my heart, cracking it,

Break too.

Alas!
Oh, loosen my corset, or my heart, thumping against it,
might break too.

First Lord
What fit is this, good lady?

What is the matter, good lady?

PAULINA
What studied torments, tyrant, hast for me?

What wheels? racks? fires? what flaying? boiling?
In leads or oils? what old or newer torture
Must I receive, whose every word deserves
To taste of thy most worst? Thy tyranny
Together working with thy jealousies,
Fancies too weak for boys, too green and idle

For girls of nine, O, think what they have done
And then run mad indeed, stark mad! for all
Thy by-gone fooleries were but spices of it.
That thou betray'dst Polixenes,'twas nothing;
That did but show thee, of a fool, inconstant
And damnable ingrateful: nor was't much,
Thou wouldst have poison'd good Camillo's honour,
To have him kill a king: poor trespasses,
More monstrous standing by: whereof I reckon
The casting forth to crows thy baby-daughter
To be or none or little; though a devil
Would have shed water out of fire ere done't:

Nor is't directly laid to thee, the death
Of the young prince, whose honourable thoughts,

What carefully planned tortures, tyrant, have you for me?
What wheels, racks, fires, flaying, boiling in lead or oil? What old or new torture
must I receive, when my every word deserves
to get me your worst? Your tyranny,
working alongside your jealousy
(which would have been silly in a boy, innocent and stupid
in a girl of nine), think what they have done,
and then go mad: stark mad! For all
your past stupidities were just a taster.
That you betrayed Polixenes, that was nothing;
that just showed that you were a fool, disloyal
and damnably ungrateful: nor was it much
that you would have ruined good Camillo's honour
by making him kill a king; tiny sins,
with a monstrous one waiting: compared to which
throwing your baby daughter out for the crows
is nothing, or little, even though a devil
would have cried tears from his fiery eyes before he would have done it:
nor can you directly be blamed for the death
of the young prince, whose honourable thoughts

Thoughts high for one so tender, cleft the heart
That could conceive a gross and foolish sire
Blemish'd his gracious dam: this is not, no,

Laid to thy answer: but the last,--O lords,
When I have said, cry 'woe!' the queen, the queen,

The sweet'st, dear'st creature's dead,

and vengeance for't
Not dropp'd down yet.

First Lord
The higher powers forbid!

PAULINA
I say she's dead; I'll swear't. If word nor oath

Prevail not, go and see: if you can bring
Tincture or lustre in her lip, her eye,
Heat outwardly or breath within, I'll serve you
As I would do the gods. But, O thou tyrant!
Do not repent these things, for they are heavier

Than all thy woes can stir; therefore betake thee

To nothing but despair. A thousand knees
Ten thousand years together, naked, fasting,
Upon a barren mountain and still winter
In storm perpetual, could not move the gods
To look that way thou wert.

LEONTES
Go on, go on :
Thou canst not speak too much; I have deserved
All tongues to talk their bitterest.

First Lord
Say no more:
Howe'er the business goes, you have made fault
I' the boldness of your speech.

PAULINA
I am sorry for't:
All faults I make, when I shall come to know them,
I do repent. Alas! I have show'd too much
The rashness of a woman: he is touch'd
To the noble heart. What's gone and what's past help

(great thoughts for one so young) split his heart,
knowing that he had such a horrid and foolish father
who could insult his gracious mother: no, the blame
for this
is not laid at your feet: but the last thing–oh lords,
when I have told you, cry out with sadness!–the
queen, the queen,
the sweetest, dearest creature is dead: and
punishment for it
has not yet arrived.

May heaven forbid it!

I tell you she is dead; I'll swear to it. If words or
oaths
are not enough, go and see: if you can bring
colour or shine to her lip, her eye,
heat outside or breath within, I'll worship you
as if you were a god. But you, you tyrant!
Don't try and ask for forgiveness, these things are
worse
than all your penitence could make up for; give
yourself up
to despair. A thousand people praying
for ten thousand years at a stretch, naked, fasting,
upon the bare mountainside in an everlasting
winter storm, could not persuade the gods
to offer you forgiveness.

Go on, go on:
you can't say enough; I deserve
the worst censure of every tongue.

Say no more:
whatever has happened, you should not
speak this way to a king.

I apologise for it:
everything I do wrong, when I find out about it,
I repent. Alas! I have shown too much
of a woman's passion: he is wounded
to the noble heart. What's gone and can't be changed

60

Should be past grief: do not receive affliction
At my petition; I beseech you, rather
Let me be punish'd, that have minded you
Of what you should forget. Now, good my liege
Sir, royal sir, forgive a foolish woman:
The love I bore your queen--lo, fool again!--
I'll speak of her no more, nor of your children;
I'll not remember you of my own lord,
Who is lost too: take your patience to you,
And I'll say nothing.

LEONTES
Thou didst speak but well
When most the truth; which I receive much better

Than to be pitied of thee. Prithee, bring me
To the dead bodies of my queen and son:
One grave shall be for both: upon them shall
The causes of their death appear, unto
Our shame perpetual. Once a day I'll visit
The chapel where they lie, and tears shed there
Shall be my recreation: so long as nature
Will bear up with this exercise, so long
I daily vow to use it. Come and lead me
Unto these sorrows.

Exeunt

can't be grieved over. Don't be wounded
by my speech; I beg you, instead
punish me, for reminding you
of what you should forget. Now, my good King,
sir, royal sir, forgive a foolish woman:
the love I had for your queen–oh, stupid again!
I'll say no more about her, nor about your children:
I'll not remind you of my own husband
(who is also lost): pull yourself together,
and I'll say nothing.

You were speaking well
when you were being most truthful; I'd rather hear that
than have your pity. Please, take me
to the dead bodies of my queen and son:
they shall share a grave: the cause of their death
will be written on their tombstones, to
my eternal shame. I'll visit the chapel where they lie
every day, and crying at their tomb
shall be my pastime: I vow that I shall do this daily
for as long as nature allows me to do it.

Lead me to these sorrows.

Scene 3

SCENE III. Bohemia. A desert country near the sea.

Enter ANTIGONUS with a Child, and a Mariner

ANTIGONUS
Thou art perfect then, our ship hath touch'd upon
The deserts of Bohemia?

*You are certain then that we have arrived at
the coast of Bohemia?*

Mariner
Ay, my lord: and fear
We have landed in ill time: the skies look grimly

*Yes, my lord: and I fear
that we have landed at a bad time: the skies look
grim*

And threaten present blusters. In my conscience,
The heavens with that we have in hand are angry
And frown upon 's.

*and threaten storms shortly. It's my belief
that the heavens are angry with what we're doing
and frown on us.*

ANTIGONUS
Their sacred wills be done! Go, get aboard;
Look to thy bark: I'll not be long before
I call upon thee.

*May their sacred will be done! Go, get on board;
get the ship ready: it won't be long before
I'll call for you.*

Mariner
Make your best haste, and go not
Too far i' the land: 'tis like to be loud weather;
Besides, this place is famous for the creatures
Of prey that keep upon't.

*Be as quick as you can, and don't go
too far inland: there's rough weather coming;
besides, this place is notorious for the creatures
of prey which live here.*

ANTIGONUS
Go thou away:
I'll follow instantly.

*You go away:
I'll be right behind you.*

Mariner
I am glad at heart
To be so rid o' the business.

*Nothing makes me happier
than to leave this business.*

Exit

ANTIGONUS
Come, poor babe:
I have heard, but not believed,

*Come on, poor baby:
I have heard, though not believed, that the spirits of
the dead*

the spirits o' the dead
May walk again: if such thing be, thy mother
Appear'd to me last night, for ne'er was dream
So like a waking. To me comes a creature,

*can walk again: if this is true, your mother
appeared to me last night; I never had a dream
that seemed so real. A creature came to me,*

Sometimes her head on one side, some another;

I never saw a vessel of like sorrow,
So fill'd and so becoming: in pure white robes,
Like very sanctity, she did approach
My cabin where I lay; thrice bow'd before me,
And gasping to begin some speech, her eyes
Became two spouts: the fury spent, anon

Did this break-from her: 'Good Antigonus,
Since fate, against thy better disposition,
Hath made thy person for the thrower-out
Of my poor babe, according to thine oath,
Places remote enough are in Bohemia,
There weep and leave it crying; and, for the babe
Is counted lost for ever, Perdita,
I prithee, call't. For this ungentle business
Put on thee by my lord, thou ne'er shalt see

Thy wife Paulina more.' And so, with shrieks
She melted into air. Affrighted much,
I did in time collect myself and thought
This was so and no slumber. Dreams are toys:
Yet for this once, yea, superstitiously,
I will be squared by this. I do believe
Hermione hath suffer'd death, and that
Apollo would, this being indeed the issue
Of King Polixenes, it should here be laid,
Either for life or death, upon the earth
Of its right father. Blossom, speed thee well!
There lie, and there thy character: there these;

Which may, if fortune please, both breed thee, pretty,
And still rest thine. The storm begins; poor wretch,

That for thy mother's fault art thus exposed
To loss and what may follow! Weep I cannot,

But my heart bleeds; and most accursed am I
To be by oath enjoin'd to this. Farewell!
The day frowns more and more: thou'rt like to have
A lullaby too rough: I never saw
The heavens so dim by day. A savage clamour!
Well may I get aboard! This is the chase:
I am gone for ever.

Exit, pursued by a bear

sometimes with her head on one side, sometimes on another;
I never saw such a sad sight,
so pure and so beautiful: in pure white robes,
like something sacred, she approached
my cabin where I lay: bowed before me three times,
and, trying to get breath for a speech, her eyes
became two fountains; when that had passed, eventually
she said this: 'Good Antigonus,
since fate, against your better judgement,
has made you the person who will exile
my poor baby, according your oath,
there are enough remote places in Bohemia;
cry there, and leave it crying: and as
the baby is lost forever, I beg you to name it
Perdita. Because of this horrible business,
which my husband forced on you, you shall never see
your wife Paulina again.' And so, screaming,
she vanished into thin air. Very frightened,
I eventually pulled myself together, and thought
that this was reality, not sleep. Dreams can deceive
but this once, superstitiously,
I will follow their direction. I do believe
that Hermione has died; and that
Apollo orders, as this is indeed the child
of King Polixenes, that it should be placed here,
either to live or die, in the land
of its real father. Little one, good luck!
There you lie, and there is a written account of you: here are things,
which may, with luck, pay for your upbringing, pretty one,
and still have some left over for you. The storm is beginning: poor wretch,
you are exposed like this due to your mother's sin,
risking destruction and whatever else may come! I cannot weep,
but my heart bleeds; it is terrible
that my oath forces me to do this. Farewell!
The day is getting blacker: it seems you will have
a rough lullaby: I never saw
such dark skies in the day. A wild racket!
I must get back on board! Here comes the hunt:
I'm leaving for good!

Enter a Shepherd

Shepherd
I would there were no age between sixteen and

three-and-twenty, or that youth would sleep out the

rest; for there is nothing in the between but
getting wenches with child, wronging the ancientry,
stealing, fighting--Hark you now! Would any but
these boiled brains of nineteen and two-and-twenty
hunt this weather? They have scared away two of my
best sheep, which I fear the wolf will sooner find

than the master: if any where I have them, 'tis by
the seaside, browsing of ivy. Good luck, an't be thy

will what have we here! Mercy on 's, a barne a very

pretty barne! A boy or a child, I wonder? A
pretty one; a very pretty one: sure, some 'scape:

though I am not bookish, yet I can read
waiting-gentlewoman in the 'scape. This has been

some stair-work, some trunk-work, some
behind-door-work: they were warmer that got this

than the poor thing is here. I'll take it up for

pity: yet I'll tarry till my son come; he hallooed

but even now. Whoa, ho, hoa!

Enter Clown

Clown
Hilloa, loa!

Shepherd
What, art so near? If thou'lt see a thing to talk
on when thou art dead and rotten, come hither.
What
ailest thou, man?

*I wish that there was nothing between the age of ten
and twenty-
three, or that young people would sleep through that
period;
for they do nothing in that time but get
girls pregnant, insult their elders, steal, fight–
listen to this! Would anyone but these
lunatics of nineteen and twenty-two hunt
in this weather? They have scared away two of my
best
sheep, which I fear the wolf will find before the
master does:
if I'll find them anywhere it will be by the seashore,
grazing on ivy. [Seeing the baby] Good heavens,
what
are you doing, what have we here? Mercy me, a
baby!
A very pretty baby! A boy or girl, I wonder?
A pretty one; a very pretty one. Somebody's been in
trouble:
although I am not educated, I can see when a lady
in waiting has got into trouble. Somebody's been
going up the back stairs,
hiding in trunks, hiding behind doors:
when they conceived this they were a good deal
warmer than the
poor thing is here. I'll take it in out of pity: but I'll
wait until
my son comes; he called just now. Hello, hello,
hello!*

Helloalo!

*What, you're so close? If you'd like to see a thing
you'll talk about the rest of your life, come here.
What
is wrong with you, man?*

Clown
I have seen two such sights, by sea and by land!

but I am not to say it is a sea, for it is now the

sky: betwixt the firmament and it you cannot thrust a bodkin's point.

I have seen two incredible sights, on the sea and land!
But I can't really say it's the sea, because it's now the sky:
you can't see a jot of difference between the two.

Shepherd
Why, boy, how is it?

Well, boy, what is it?

Clown
I would you did but see how it chafes, how it rages, how it takes up the shore! but that's not the point. O, the most piteous cry of the poor souls! sometimes to see 'em, and not to see 'em; now the

ship boring the moon with her main-mast, and anon

swallowed with yest and froth, as you'ld thrust a cork into a hogshead. And then for the land-service, to see how the bear tore out his shoulder-bone; how he cried to me for help and said his name was Antigonus, a nobleman. But to make an end of the ship, to see how the sea flap-dragoned

it: but, first, how the poor souls roared, and the sea mocked them; and how the poor gentleman roared
and the bear mocked him, both roaring louder than

the sea or weather.

I wish you could see how it boils, how it rages, how it smashes on the shore! But that's not the point. Oh, the awful cry of the poor souls! Sometimes I saw them, sometimes I didn't; one minute
the ship seemed to be jabbing at the moon with her mast, and then
the next swallowed in froth and bubbles, like a cork in a beer barrel. And as for what happened on land, I saw
the bear tear out his shoulder bone, and he cried to me for help and said his name was Antigonus, a nobleman. But I must finish telling you about the ship, about how
the sea swallowed it: but first, how the poor souls roared, and the sea mockingly copied them, and the poor
gentleman roared, and the bear mockingly copied him,
both of them roaring louder than the sea or the weather.

Shepherd
Name of mercy, when was this, boy?

Good heavens, when was this, boy?

Clown
Now, now: I have not winked since I saw these sights: the men are not yet cold under water, nor the bear half dined on the gentleman: he's at it now.

Just now: just a blink of an eye ago:
the men are not yet cold under the water, nor has the bear finished half the gentleman: he's eating now.

Shepherd
Would I had been by, to have helped the old man!

I wish I had been there, to help the old man!

Clown
I would you had been by the ship side, to have

I wish you'd been by the ship, to have

helped her: there your charity would have lacked
footing.

saved her: but your bravery would have been sunk.

Shepherd
Heavy matters! heavy matters! but look thee here,
boy. Now bless thyself: thou mettest with things
dying, I with things newborn. Here's a sight for

thee; look thee, a bearing-cloth for a squire's
child! look thee here; take up, take up, boy;
open't. So, let's see: it was told me I should be
rich by the fairies. This is some changeling:
open't. What's within, boy?

Great matters! Great matters! But you look here,
boy. Now bless yourself: you have seen things
dying, I have found something newborn. Here's a
site for
you; look at that, a quality baptismal robe!
Look here; pick it up, pick it up, boy;
open it. So, let's see: the fairies once told me
that I would be rich. This is a changeling:
open it up. What's inside, boy?

Clown
You're a made old man: if the sins of your youth

are forgiven you, you're well to live. Gold! all gold!

You're made for life old man: if the sins of your
youth
don't catch up with you, you will have a great life.
Gold! All gold!

Shepherd
This is fairy gold, boy, and 'twill prove so: up
with't, keep it close: home, home, the next way.
We are lucky, boy; and to be so still requires

nothing but secrecy. Let my sheep go: come, good
boy, the next way home.

This is fairy gold, boy, you shall see: pick it up,
hold it tight: home, home, the quickest way.
We are lucky, boy; to keep our luck we need do
nothing
but keep this secret. Forget about the sheep: come,
good boy, let's take the quickest way home.

Clown
Go you the next way with your findings. I'll go see

if the bear be gone from the gentleman and how
much
he hath eaten: they are never curst but when they
are hungry: if there be any of him left, I'll bury
it.

You go the quickest way with your discoveries. I'll
go and see
if the bear has left the gentleman yet and how much
he has eaten: they are only ever vicious when they
are hungry: if there is any of him left, I'll bury
it.

Shepherd
That's a good deed. If thou mayest discern by that

which is left of him what he is, fetch me to the
sight of him.

That will be a good deed. If there's enough of him
left
to tell who he is, call me to see him.

Clown
Marry, will I; and you shall help to put him i' the ground . *Yes, I will; you can help me to bury him.*

Shepherd
'Tis a lucky day, boy, and we'll do good deeds on't. *This is our lucky day, boy, and we should do good*

deeds.

Exeunt

Act 4

Scene 1

SCENE I. Enter Time, the Chorus

Time
I, that please some, try all, both joy and terror
Of good and bad, that makes and unfolds error,
Now take upon me, in the name of Time,
To use my wings. Impute it not a crime
To me or my swift passage, that I slide
O'er sixteen years and leave the growth untried
Of that wide gap, since it is in my power

To o'erthrow law and in one self-born hour
To plant and o'erwhelm custom. Let me pass
The same I am, ere ancient'st order was
Or what is now received: I witness to
The times that brought them in; so shall I do
To the freshest things now reigning and make stale
The glistering of this present, as my tale
Now seems to it. Your patience this allowing,
I turn my glass and give my scene such growing
As you had slept between: Leontes leaving,

The effects of his fond jealousies so grieving

That he shuts up himself, imagine me,
Gentle spectators, that I now may be
In fair Bohemia, and remember well,
I mentioned a son o' the king's, which Florizel
I now name to you; and with speed so pace

To speak of Perdita, now grown in grace

Equal with wondering: what of her ensues

I list not prophecy; but let Time's news
Be known when 'tis brought forth.
A shepherd's daughter,
And what to her adheres, which follows after,
Is the argument of Time. Of this allow,
If ever you have spent time worse ere now;
If never, yet that Time himself doth say

He wishes earnestly you never may.

Exit

I please some, and test all: both joy and terror,
good and bad, errors committed and undone,
I will now take on, in the name of time,
and spread my wings. Do not be cross
with me, or my swift journey, if I slide
over sixteen years, and do not try to show
what happened in that time, because it is within my power
to overthrow the law, and in one hour I've made
I can create and demolish customs. Let me go,
I am the same as I was before the world began
as in these modern times. I have seen
the times when they began; and I shall see
the things of this very moment
grow old, as my tale now does.
If you will allow this,
I turn the glass over, and let the scene change
as if you had slept through the interim: abandoning Leontes,
who is so upset at the results of his foolish jealousy

that he has shut himself away, imagine,
sweet audience, that I'm now
in fair Bohemia, and remember
that a son of the king's was mentioned earlier, whom
I can now tell you is called Florizel; now let's rush on
to talk of Perdita, who has now developed a loveliness
which equals the admiration it causes. What happens to her
I shan't tell you; let the news of time

be seen when it happens. A shepherd's daughter,
and what happens to her, which is what is following
is what Time wants to show you. Allow this, whether
or not you have ever spent time less agreeably,
Time only wishes with all his heart that you never will.

Scene 2

SCENE II. Bohemia. The palace of POLIXENES.

Enter POLIXENES and CAMILLO

POLIXENES
I pray thee, good Camillo, be no more importunate:
'tis a sickness denying thee any thing; a death to
grant this.

*Please, good Camillo, stop asking me:
it makes me ill to deny you anything; it would kill me
to give you this.*

CAMILLO
It is fifteen years since I saw my country: though
I have for the most part been aired abroad, I

desire to lay my bones there. Besides, the penitent
king, my master, hath sent for me; to whose feeling

sorrows I might be some allay, or I o'erween to
think so, which is another spur to my departure.

*It is fifteen years since I saw my country: though
since then I have mostly been breathing foreign air,
I
would like to be buried there. Besides, the penitent
king, my master, has sent for me; and I might be
able
to give him some comfort in his sorrow, or I presume
I can, which is another reason to want to go.*

POLIXENES
As thou lovest me, Camillo, wipe not out the rest of
thy services by leaving me now: the need I have of
thee thine own goodness hath made; better not to

have had thee than thus to want thee: thou, having

made me businesses which none without thee can

sufficiently manage, must either stay to execute

them thyself or take away with thee the very
services thou hast done; which if I have not enough

considered, as too much I cannot, to be more

thankful to thee shall be my study, and my profit

therein the heaping friendships. Of that fatal
country, Sicilia, prithee speak no more; whose very
naming punishes me with the remembrance of that

*As you love me, Camillo, don't wipe out everything
you've done for me by leaving me now: you have
made me come to rely on you through your own
goodness;
it would be better not to have had you, than to lose
you:
you have started things for me which only you can
finish,
you must either stay and do them yourself, or
destroy
all the good things that you have done: if I haven't
rewarded you enough (I can never reward you
enough), I shall
learn how to be more grateful; and the profit I get
from that
would be more of your friendly services. Please
don't speak any more
of that fateful country, Sicily; the very name of it

hurts me with the memory of that penitent*

70

penitent, as thou callest him, and reconciled king, my brother; whose loss of his most precious queen and children are even now to be afresh lamented. Say to me, when sawest thou the Prince Florizel, my son? Kings are no less unhappy, their issue not

being gracious, than they are in losing them when they have approved their virtues.

(as you call him) and reconciled King, my brother; the loss of his most precious queen and children are still being mourned. Tell me, when did you last see Prince Florizel, my son? Kings are just as unhappy when their children are not good, as they are if they lose them when they know that they are good.

CAMILLO

Sir, it is three days since I saw the prince. What his happier affairs may be, are to me unknown: but I have missingly noted, he is of late much retired from court and is less frequent to his princely exercises than formerly he hath appeared.

Sir, it is three days since I saw the prince. What he has to do that is more important, I don't know: but he has been conspicuous by his absence recently from the court and does not undertake his princely exercises as often as he used it.

POLIXENES

I have considered so much, Camillo, and with some care; so far that I have eyes under my service which look upon his removedness; from whom I have this intelligence, that he is seldom from the house of a most homely shepherd; a man, they say, that from very nothing, and beyond the imagination of his neighbours, is grown into an unspeakable estate.

I have thought about this, Camillo, and with some care; so much so that I have spies watching him when he is away; they have given me reports that he is seldom away from the house of a very lowly shepherd; a man, they say, that started with absolutely nothing, and has acquired a vast fortune, which his neighbours can't explain.

CAMILLO

I have heard, sir, of such a man, who hath a daughter of most rare note: the report of her is extended more than can be thought to begin from such a cottage.

I have heard about such a man, sir, who has a quite remarkable daughter: the reports of her would seem to indicate she is far more remarkable than one would expect from such a cottage.

POLIXENES

That's likewise part of my intelligence; but, I fear, the angle that plucks our son thither. Thou shalt accompany us to the place; where we will, not appearing what we are, have some question with the shepherd; from whose simplicity I think it not uneasy to get the cause of my son's resort thither. Prithee, be my present partner in this business, and lay aside the thoughts of Sicilia.

That's what I've been told too; but, I fear, she is the hook that draws my son there. You will come with me to the place; there we will, without revealing who we are, speak with the shepherd; I think we should easily be able to elicit from the simple fellow why my son goes there. Please, help me manage this business, and forget about Sicily.

CAMILLO

I willingly obey your command.

I willingly do as you say.

POLIXENES

My best Camillo! We must disguise ourselves.

My splendid Camillo! We must disguise ourselves.

Exeunt

Scene 3

SCENE III. A road near the Shepherd's cottage.

Enter AUTOLYCUS, singing

AUTOLYCUS

When daffodils begin to peer,	*When daffodils begin to appear*
With heigh! the doxy over the dale,	*the beggar woman comes over the fields*
Why, then comes in the sweet o' the year;	*then comes the sweet time of the year*
For the red blood reigns in the winter's pale.	*when red blood colours the white cheeks of winter.*
The white sheet bleaching on the hedge,	*White sheets drying on the hedge,*
With heigh! the sweet birds, O, how they sing!	*hey, the sweet birds, how they sing!*
Doth set my pugging tooth on edge;	*Set my thieving teeth on edge;*
For a quart of ale is a dish for a king.	*a quart of ale is a dish for a king.*
The lark, that tirra-lyra chants,	*The lark that sings its warbling song,*
With heigh! with heigh! the thrush and the jay,	*hey! Hey! The thrush and the jay*
Are summer songs for me and my aunts,	*sing the summer songs for me and my girls*
While we lie tumbling in the hay.	*as we lie tumbling in the hay.*
I have served Prince Florizel and in my time	*I have been in the service of Prince Florizel, and in my time have worn*
wore three-pile; but now I am out of service:	*thick velvet, but now I have no job.*
But shall I go mourn for that, my dear?	*But shall I let that make me sad?*
The pale moon shines by night:	*The pale moon shines at night:*
And when I wander here and there,	*and when I wander here and there*
I then do most go right.	*that's the life for me.*
If tinkers may have leave to live,	*If tinkers are allowed to live*
And bear the sow-skin budget,	*and carry their pigskin bags*
Then my account I well may, give,	*then I will stand up for myself*
And in the stocks avouch it.	*even in the stocks.*
My traffic is sheets; when the kite builds, look to	*My trade is stealing sheets; when the kite is building his nest*
lesser linen. My father named me Autolycus; who	*you must look out for your small linen. My father named me Autolycus;*
being, as I am, littered under Mercury, was likewise	*being who I am, born under Mercury, I am also*
a snapper-up of unconsidered trifles. With die and	*a thief of neglected things. Through dice and women I got*
drab I purchased this caparison, and my revenue is	*this outfit, and I get my living through*
the silly cheat. Gallows and knock are too powerful	*petty trickery. The gallows and beatings are too common*
on the highway: beating and hanging are terrors to	*on the highway: beating and hanging terrify me:*
me: for the life to come, I sleep out the thought	*as for the future, I don't worry about it.*
of it. A prize! a prize!	*Now, there's a prize!*

Enter Clown

Clown

Let me see: every 'leven wether tods; every tod

yields pound and odd shilling; fifteen hundred
shorn. what comes the wool to?

Let me see: every eleven fleeces makes a tod; every tod
pays a pound and a shilling; fifteen hundred
sheep sheared, how much does that come to?

AUTOLYCUS
[Aside]
If the springe hold, the cock's mine.

If the trap works, this bird is mine.

Clown
I cannot do't without counters. Let me see; what am
I to buy for our sheep-shearing feast? Three pound

of sugar, five pound of currants, rice,--what will
this sister of mine do with rice? But my father
hath made her mistress of the feast, and she lays it
on. She hath made me four and twenty nose-gays for
the shearers, three-man-song-men all, and very good
ones; but they are most of them means and bases;
but
one puritan amongst them, and he sings psalms to

horn-pipes. I must have saffron to colour the warden

pies; mace; dates?--none, that's out of my note;
nutmegs, seven; a race or two of ginger, but that I

may beg; four pound of prunes, and as many of
raisins o' the sun.

I need an abacus for it. Let me see; what should
I buy for our sheep shearing celebrations? Three pounds
of sugar, five pounds of currents, rice–what does
that sister of my mine want with rice? But my father
has put her in charge of the feast, and she does it
well. She has made me twenty-four bouquets for
the shearers, all harmonious singers, and very good
ones; but most of them are tenors and basses; there
is only
one treble amongst them and he's a puritan who
sings psalms
accompanied by the hornpipe. I must have saffron to
colour the apple pies;
mace; dates, no no dates–that's not on my list; seven
nutmegs; one or two ginger roots, but I can
scrounge those;
four pounds of prunes, and the same of sun-dried
raisins.

AUTOLYCUS
O that ever I was born!

Alas that I was ever born!

Grovelling on the ground

Clown
I' the name of me!

Well, for the life of me!

AUTOLYCUS
O, help me, help me! pluck but off these rags; and
then, death, death!

Oh, help me, help me! Just tear off these rags; and
then, give me death, death!

Clown
Alack, poor soul! thou hast need of more rags to lay
on thee, rather than have these off.

Alas, poor soul! You need more rags to put
round you, rather than take these ones off.

AUTOLYCUS

O sir, the loathsomeness of them offends me more
than the stripes I have received, which are mighty
ones and millions.

*Oh sir, their foulness upsets me more
than the blows I have been given, of which
I've had millions of severe ones.*

Clown
Alas, poor man! a million of beating may come to a
great matter.

*Alas, poor man! A million beatings is a
serious business.*

AUTOLYCUS
I am robbed, sir, and beaten; my money and apparel

*I have been robbed, sir, and beaten; my money and
clothes*

ta'en from me, and these detestable things put upon
me.

taken from me, and these horrible things put on me.

Clown
What, by a horseman, or a footman?

Was the robber mounted or on foot?

AUTOLYCUS
A footman, sweet sir, a footman.

He was a footpad, sweet sir, a footpad.

Clown
Indeed, he should be a footman by the garments he

*Indeed, these garments he has left with you show
that*

has left with thee: if this be a horseman's coat,
it hath seen very hot service. Lend me thy hand,
I'll help thee: come, lend me thy hand.

*he was a footpad: if this is the coat of a horseman
it's seen a lot of service. Give me your hand,
I'll help you: come on, give me your hand.*

AUTOLYCUS
O, good sir, tenderly, O!

Oh, good sir, gently, oh!

Clown
Alas, poor soul!

Alas, poor soul!

AUTOLYCUS
O, good sir, softly, good sir! I fear, sir, my
shoulder-blade is out.

*Oh, good sir, gently, good sir! I fear, sir, I've
dislocated my collarbone.*

Clown
How now! canst stand?

How's that! Can you stand?

AUTOLYCUS
[Picking his pocket]
Softly, dear sir; good sir, softly. You ha' done me
a charitable office.

*Gently, dear sir; dear sir, gently. You have done me
a great favour.*

Clown

Dost lack any money? I have a little money for thee. *Have you no money? I can give you a little.*

AUTOLYCUS
No, good sweet sir; no, I beseech you, sir: I have
a kinsman not past three quarters of a mile hence,

unto whom I was going; I shall there have money,
or
any thing I want: offer me no money, I pray you;
that kills my heart.

*No, good sweet sir; no, I beg you, sir: I have
kinsman not more than three quarters of a mile
away,
whom I was going to see; he should give me money,
or
anything I want: please don't offer me any money;
that would break my heart.*

Clown
What manner of fellow was he that robbed you?

What sort of chap was the one who robbed you?

AUTOLYCUS
A fellow, sir, that I have known to go about with
troll-my-dames; I knew him once a servant of the
prince: I cannot tell, good sir, for which of his
virtues it was, but he was certainly whipped out of
the court.

*A fellow, sir, whom I have seen running a booth
at the fair; I know that he was once a servant of the
prince: I don't know, good sir, which of his virtues
it was for, but he was certainly whipped out of the
court.*

Clown
His vices, you would say; there's no virtue whipped
out of the court: they cherish it to make it stay
there; and yet it will no more but abide.

*His vices, you should say; they don't whip virtue
out of the court: they love to keep it
there; but it only stops for a moment.*

AUTOLYCUS
Vices, I would say, sir. I know this man well: he

hath been since an ape-bearer; then a
process-server, a bailiff; then he compassed a
motion of the Prodigal Son, and married a tinker's

wife within a mile where my land and living lies;

and, having flown over many knavish professions, he
settled only in rogue: some call him Autolycus.

*Yes, I should say vices, sir. I know this man well:
since
then he has been a monkey trainer; then a
process server, a bailiff;
then he acquired a puppet show about the prodigal
son,
and married a tinker's wife within a mile of my land
and estate;
and, having tried many dodgy professions, he
took up villainy: some call him Autolycus.*

Clown
Out upon him! prig, for my life, prig: he haunts

wakes, fairs and bear-baitings.

*Damn him! A tinker and a thief, I swear: he hangs
around
festivals, fairs and the bear baiting.*

AUTOLYCUS
Very true, sir; he, sir, he; that's the rogue that
put me into this apparel.

*Very true, sir; him, sir, him; that's the scoundrel who
dressed me like this.*

Clown
Not a more cowardly rogue in all Bohemia: if you had
but looked big and spit at him, he'ld have run.

There is no more cowardly rascal in all of Bohemia: if you had
just stood tall and spat at him, he'd have run away.

AUTOLYCUS
I must confess to you, sir, I am no fighter: I am
false of heart that way; and that he knew, I warrant

him.

I must confess to you, sir, I am not a fighter: I am
a terrible coward in that way; and I'm sure that he knew
that.

Clown
How do you now?

How are you now?

AUTOLYCUS
Sweet sir, much better than I was; I can stand and
walk: I will even take my leave of you, and pace
softly towards my kinsman's.

Dear sir, much better than I was; I can stand and
walk: I will now say goodbye, and walk
gently to my kinsman's.

Clown
Shall I bring thee on the way?

Do you want me to come with you?

AUTOLYCUS
No, good-faced sir; no, sweet sir.

No, kind faced sir; no, sweet sir.

Clown
Then fare thee well: I must go buy spices for our
sheep-shearing.

Then goodbye: I must go and buy spices for our
sheep shearing festival.

AUTOLYCUS
Prosper you, sweet sir!

May you be blessed, sweet sir!

Exit Clown
Your purse is not hot enough to purchase your spice.
I'll be with you at your sheep-shearing too: if I
make not this cheat bring out another and the
shearers prove sheep, let me be unrolled and my name
put in the book of virtue!

There's not enough in your purse to buy your spices.
I'll come to your sheep shearing too; if I
can't make this trick lead on to another and
fleece those shearers, let me be struck off
the thieves' register and my name
be written in the book of good men!

Sings
Jog on, jog on, the foot-path way,
And merrily hent the stile-a:
A merry heart goes all the day,
Your sad tires in a mile-a.

Jog on, jog on, along the footpath,
and merrily jump the stile:
a merry heart can go all day,
the sad heart tires in a mile.

Exit

Scene 4

SCENE IV. The Shepherd's cottage.

Enter FLORIZEL and PERDITA

FLORIZEL
These your unusual weeds to each part of you
Do give a life: no shepherdess, but Flora

Peering in April's front. This your sheep-shearing
Is as a meeting of the petty gods,
And you the queen on't.

These unusual clothes of yours enhance
every aspect of your beauty: not a shepherdess but
the goddess Flora
bringing in the spring. This sheep shearing of yours
is like a meeting of the minor gods,
with you as their queen.

PERDITA
Sir, my gracious lord,
To chide at your extremes it not becomes me:
O, pardon, that I name them! Your high self,
The gracious mark o' the land, you have obscured

With a swain's wearing, and me, poor lowly maid,
Most goddess-like prank'd up: but that our feasts
In every mess have folly and the feeders
Digest it with a custom, I should blush
To see you so attired, swoon, I think,

To show myself a glass.

Sir, my gracious lord,
it's not my place to criticise what you do:
excuse me for even mentioning it! You have covered
up your great dignity, the person everyone looks up
to,
with a peasant's clothes, and I, insignificant girl,
am got up like a goddess: if not for the fact that
our celebrations have foolishness everywhere and
everyone joins in with relish, I would be ashamed
to see you dress like this, and I would faint from
embarrassment
if I saw myself in the mirror.

FLORIZEL
I bless the time
When my good falcon made her flight across
Thy father's ground.

I bless the time
when the wings of my fate
brought me to your father's land.

PERDITA
Now Jove afford you cause!
To me the difference forges dread; your greatness

Hath not been used to fear. Even now I tremble
To think your father, by some accident,
Should pass this way as you did: O, the Fates!
How would he look, to see his work so noble
Vilely bound up? What would he say? Or how

Now may Jove give you reason to!
The difference in our rank worries me; you're so
high
you're not used to fear. Even now I am trembling
to think that your father, through some mischance,
might come this way just as you did: oh, the luck!
What would he think, if he saw his noble offspring
dressed so shabbily? Or what would you say? And

Should I, in these my borrow'd flaunts, behold
The sternness of his presence?

FLORIZEL
Apprehend
Nothing but jollity. The gods themselves,
Humbling their deities to love, have taken
The shapes of beasts upon them: Jupiter
Became a bull, and bellow'd; the green Neptune
A ram, and bleated; and the fire-robed god,
Golden Apollo, a poor humble swain,
As I seem now. Their transformations
Were never for a piece of beauty rarer,
Nor in a way so chaste, since my desires
Run not before mine honour, nor my lusts
Burn hotter than my faith.

PERDITA
O, but, sir,
Your resolution cannot hold, when 'tis
Opposed, as it must be, by the power of the king:
One of these two must be necessities,
Which then will speak, that you must
change this purpose,
Or I my life.

FLORIZEL
Thou dearest Perdita,
With these forced thoughts, I prithee, darken not
The mirth o' the feast. Or I'll be thine, my fair,

Or not my father's. For I cannot be
Mine own, nor any thing to any, if
I be not thine. To this I am most constant,
Though destiny say no. Be merry, gentle;
Strangle such thoughts as these with any thing
That you behold the while. Your guests are coming:
Lift up your countenance, as it were the day
Of celebration of that nuptial which
We two have sworn shall come.

PERDITA
O lady Fortune,
Stand you auspicious!

FLORIZEL
See, your guests approach:

how
would I, in this borrowed finery, cope with
his majestic presence?

Look forward
to nothing but fun. The gods themselves
have taken on the shapes of animals,
humbling their divinity to find love: Jupiter
became a bellowing bull; Neptune from the sea
became a ram and bleated; and the fire clad god,
Golden Apollo, became a poor humble shepherd,
as I am now. They never changed themselves
for such a wonderful beauty,
and they were not as chaste, since my desires
do not outstrip my honour, and my lusts
are not stronger than my good faith.

Oh, but, sir,
your determination will not last when it is
opposed, as it will be, by the power of the king:
one of these two things must happen
then; you must forget your intentions
or I will lose my life.

You dear Perdita,
please don't spoil the fun of the feast
with these far-fetched thoughts: if I don't have you,
my darling,
I'll be no good to my father. I can't be
any good to myself, or do good for anyone, if
I'm not yours. I shall stick to this,
whatever destiny says. Be happy, sweet one;
push away these thoughts with all things
you can see here. Your guests are coming:
put on your best smile, as if it was
the wedding day which we have both sworn
we will come to.

Oh Lady Fortune,
smile on us!

See, your guests are coming:

78

Address yourself to entertain them sprightly,
And let's be red with mirth.

make an effort to give them a jolly welcome,
and let's laugh until we're red in the face.

Enter Shepherd, Clown, MOPSA, DORCAS, and others, with POLIXENES and CAMILLO disguised

Shepherd
Fie, daughter! when my old wife lived, upon
This day she was both pantler, butler, cook,
Both dame and servant; welcomed all, served all;

Hello, daughter! When my old wife was alive, on
this day she would be cellarman, butler, cook,
both lady and servant; she welcomed everyone,
served everyone;

Would sing her song and dance her turn; now here,
At upper end o' the table, now i' the middle;
On his shoulder, and his; her face o' fire

she would sing and dance; now here,
at the top end of the table, now in the middle;
leaning on his shoulder, then his; her face would be
red

With labour and the thing she took to quench it,

with the work, and with the drink she had to cool
down

She would to each one sip. You are retired,
As if you were a feasted one and not
The hostess of the meeting: pray you, bid
These unknown friends to's welcome; for it is

she would toast each of them. You are shy,
as if you were a guest, and not
the hostess of the gathering: please, give
these friends who are strangers to us a welcome;
that's

A way to make us better friends, more known.
Come, quench your blushes and present yourself
That which you are, mistress o' the feast: come on,
And bid us welcome to your sheep-shearing,
As your good flock shall prosper.

the way to get us better acquainted.
Come, stop blushing, and introduce yourself
as what you are, the mistress of the feast. Come on,
and welcome us to your sheep shearing,
and may your good flock prosper.

PERDITA
[To POLIXENES] Sir, welcome:
It is my father's will I should take on me
The hostess-ship o' the day.

Sir, welcome:
my father orders that I should be
the hostess for today.

To CAMILLO
You're welcome, sir.
Give me those flowers there, Dorcas. Reverend sirs,
For you there's rosemary and rue; these keep
Seeming and savour all the winter long:
Grace and remembrance be to you both,
And welcome to our shearing!

You're welcome, sir.
Dorcas, give me those flowers. Respected gentlemen,
here is rosemary and rue for you; these keep
their looks and scent all winter long:
blessings and friendship to both of you,
and welcome to our shearing!

POLIXENES
Shepherdess,
A fair one are you--well you fit our ages
With flowers of winter.

Shepherdess -
a lovely one you are--you've matched our ages nicely
with the flowers of winter.

PERDITA
Sir, the year growing ancient,
Not yet on summer's death, nor on the birth

Sir, the year is getting on,
it's not yet autumn, or the start

79

Of trembling winter, the fairest
flowers o' the season
Are our carnations and streak'd gillyvors,
Which some call nature's bastards: of that kind
Our rustic garden's barren; and I care not
To get slips of them.

of chilly winter, and the loveliest
flowers of this season
are our carnations and multicoloured gillyflowers,
which some call nature's bastards: we don't have
that sort in our rustic garden, and I don't want
to grow them.

POLIXENES
Wherefore, gentle maiden,
Do you neglect them?

Why, gentle maiden,
don't you grow them?

PERDITA
For I have heard it said
There is an art which in their piedness shares
With great creating nature.

Because I have heard it said
that their multicoloured looks
are artificially created.

POLIXENES
Say there be;
Yet nature is made better by no mean
But nature makes that mean: so, over that art
Which you say adds to nature, is an art
That nature makes. You see, sweet maid, we marry
A gentler scion to the wildest stock,
And make conceive a bark of baser kind
By bud of nobler race: this is an art
Which does mend nature, change it rather, but
The art itself is nature.

What if they are;
nature can only be made better
by things she has created herself: so
what you call artificial is in fact
made by men, who are made by nature.
You see, sweet maid, we graft
a gentle nature onto the wildest plants,
and improve the lower things
by adding the seed of a nobler race: this is an art
which corrects nature—or rather changes it—but
it is still nature.

PERDITA
So it is.

Yes it is.

POLIXENES
Then make your garden rich in gillyvors,
And do not call them bastards.

So fill your garden with gillyflowers,
and do not call them bastards.

PERDITA
I'll not put
The dibble in earth to set one slip of them;
No more than were I painted I would wish
This youth should say 'twere well and only therefore
Desire to breed by me. Here's flowers for you;

I wouldn't put
the hoe into the earth to plant a single one of them;
no more so than if I wore makeup and
this youth said he liked it and only wanted
to breed with me because of it. Here are flowers for
you;

Hot lavender, mints, savoury, marjoram;
The marigold, that goes to bed wi' the sun
And with him rises weeping: these are flowers
Of middle summer, and I think they are given
To men of middle age. You're very welcome.

hot lavender, mints, savoury, marjoram;
the marigold, which goes to sleep with the sun
and rises with the dew: these are the flowers
of the middle of summer, and I think I'm giving them
to men of middle age. You're very welcome.

CAMILLO
I should leave grazing, were I of your flock,
And only live by gazing.

If I was one of your flock I would give up grazing
and just spend my life gazing.

PERDITA
Out, alas!
You'd be so lean, that blasts of January
Would blow you through and through.
Now, my fair'st friend,
I would I had some flowers o' the spring that might
Become your time of day; and yours, and yours,
That wear upon your virgin branches yet
Your maidenheads growing: O Proserpina,
For the flowers now, that frighted thou let'st fall

From Dis's waggon! daffodils,
That come before the swallow dares, and take
The winds of March with beauty; violets dim,
But sweeter than the lids of Juno's eyes
Or Cytherea's breath; pale primroses
That die unmarried, ere they can behold
Bight Phoebus in his strength--a malady
Most incident to maids; bold oxlips and
The crown imperial; lilies of all kinds,
The flower-de-luce being one! O, these I lack,

To make you garlands of, and my sweet friend,
To strew him o'er and o'er!

Don't be so daft!
You would get so thin that the winds of January
would blow right through you. Now, my fair friends,

I wish I had some spring flowers that would
suit your age; and yours, and yours,

who are still dressed in innocence: oh Prosperina,
I wish I had the flowers that you, frightened,
dropped
from Pluto's chariot! Daffodils,
that come ahead of the swallow, and delight
the winds of March with their beauty; violets, dim,
but sweeter than the lids of Juno's eyes
or the breath of Venus; pale primroses,
that die unmarried, before they can see
the bright sun at his strongest (an illness
maids often suffer from); tall oxlips
and the Crown Imperial; lilies of all kinds,
the fleur-de-lys being one of them. Oh, I don't have
these
to make you garlands, and to cover my sweet friend
over and over!

FLORIZEL
What, like a corse?

What, like a corpse?

PERDITA
No, like a bank for love to lie and play on;
Not like a corse; or if, not to be buried,
But quick and in mine arms. Come, take your
flowers:
Methinks I play as I have seen them do
In Whitsun pastorals: sure this robe of mine
Does change my disposition.

No, like a bank for lovers to lie and play on;
not like a corpse; or if you were, not buried,
but alive and in my arms. Come, take your flowers:

I think I'm acting as I've seen them do
in the Whitsun plays: I think my dress
must have changed my character.

FLORIZEL
What you do
Still betters what is done. When you speak, sweet,
I'ld have you do it ever: when you sing,
I'ld have you buy and sell so, so give alms,

Everything you do
gets better and better. When you speak, sweet,
I wish you would never stop: when you sing,
I'd like you to do it when you're trading, giving

Pray so; and, for the ordering your affairs,

To sing them too: when you do dance, I wish you
A wave o' the sea, that you might ever do

Nothing but that; move still, still so,
And own no other function: each your doing,
So singular in each particular,
Crowns what you are doing in the present deed,
That all your acts are queens.

PERDITA
O Doricles,
Your praises are too large: but that your youth,

And the true blood which peepeth fairly through't,
Do plainly give you out an unstain'd shepherd,
With wisdom I might fear, my Doricles,
You woo'd me the false way.

FLORIZEL
I think you have
As little skill to fear as I have purpose
To put you to't. But come; our dance, I pray:
Your hand, my Perdita: so turtles pair,

That never mean to part.

PERDITA
I'll swear for 'em.

POLIXENES
This is the prettiest low-born lass that ever
Ran on the green-sward: nothing she does or seems

But smacks of something greater than herself,
Too noble for this place.

CAMILLO
He tells her something
That makes her blood look out: good sooth, she is
The queen of curds and cream.

Clown

charity,
praying; when you are giving orders for your
business
I'd like you to sing them too: when you dance, I wish
that you were a wave on the sea, that would never
do
anything but that; just keep moving, stay like that,
have nothing else to do: everything you do,
so wonderful in every way,
adds to what you are doing at the moment,
and makes everything you do heavenly.

Oh Doricles,
you give me too much praise: if it wasn't that your
youth,
and the honest blood which can be seen in you,
clearly indicate that you are an innocent shepherd,
if I thought about it I might worry, my Doricles,
that you are wooing me with falsehoods.

I think you have
as little cause to fear as I have intention
to do that. But come, let us dance please:
give me your hand, my Perdita: together like
turtledoves
that will never part.

I swear they don't.

This is the prettiest peasant lass that ever
ran in the fields: everything she does and appears to
be
makes her look as if she was nobler than her birth,
too noble for this place.

He's telling her something
that's making her blush: good heavens,
she is the queen of the dairy.

Come on, strike up!

Come on, let's have music!

DORCAS
Mopsa must be your mistress: marry, garlic,
To mend her kissing with!

*Mopsa will dance with you: give her some garlic
to make her kisses sweeter!*

MOPSA
Now, in good time!

Now, behave yourself!

Clown
Not a word, a word; we stand upon our manners.
Come, strike up!

*No talking, no talking; we're wasting time.
Come, play the music!*

Music. Here a dance of Shepherds and Shepherdesses

POLIXENES
Pray, good shepherd, what fair swain is this
Which dances with your daughter?

*Tell me, good shepherd, what handsome lad is this
who dances with your daughter?*

Shepherd
They call him Doricles; and boasts himself
To have a worthy feeding: but I have it
Upon his own report and I believe it;
He looks like sooth. He says he loves my daughter:
I think so too; for never gazed the moon
Upon the water as he'll stand and read
As 'twere my daughter's eyes: and, to be plain.

I think there is not half a kiss to choose
Who loves another best.

*They call him Doricles; he says
he owns a good estate: I have his
word on it and I believe it;
he looks honest. He says he loves my daughter:
I believe that too; for the moon never looked
down on the water in the same way as he will
stand looking into my daughter's eyes: to be honest
with you
I don't think there's any difference
in their devotion to each other.*

POLIXENES
She dances featly.

She dances beautifully.

Shepherd
So she does any thing; though I report it,
That should be silent: if young Doricles
Do light upon her, she shall bring him that
Which he not dreams of.

*She does everything beautifully, although
I say it myself: if young Doricles
chooses her, she will bring him things
he cannot dream of.*

Enter Servant

Servant
O master, if you did but hear the pedlar at the
door, you would never dance again after a tabour
and
pipe; no, the bagpipe could not move you: he sings

*Oh master, if you only heard the pedlar at the
door, you would never want to dance to the whistle
and
drum again; you wouldn't care for the bagpipes: he*

several tunes faster than you'll tell money; he
utters them as he had eaten ballads and all men's
ears grew to his tunes.

*sings
different tunes faster than you can count money; he
sings them as if he had eaten the music sheets and
everyone bends their ears to his tune.*

Clown
He could never come better; he shall come in. I
love a ballad but even too well, if it be doleful
matter merrily set down, or a very pleasant thing
indeed and sung lamentably.

*He couldn't have come at a better time; let him in.
I'm exceedingly fond of ballads, if it has a sad
subject with a merry tune, or a merry subject
set to sad music.*

Servant
He hath songs for man or woman, of all sizes; no
milliner can so fit his customers with gloves: he
has the prettiest love-songs for maids; so without
bawdry, which is strange; with such delicate

*He has songs for men and women, of all sizes;
no milliner could make a better fit with his gloves:
he has the prettiest love songs for girls; completely
without vulgarity, which is unusual; with such
delicate*

burthens of dildos and fadings, 'jump her and thump
her;' and where some stretch-mouthed rascal would,
as it were, mean mischief and break a foul gap into
the matter, he makes the maid to answer 'Whoop, do
me

*nonsensical choruses, 'jump her and thump
her;' and when some foulmouthed rascal
wants to make mischief and put some vulgarity
into the song, he has the made answer 'whoop, do
me*

no harm, good man;' puts him off, slights him, with

*no harm, good man;' pushes him away and puts him
down*

'Whoop, do me no harm, good man.'

with 'whoop, do me no harm, good man.'

POLIXENES
This is a brave fellow.

This sounds like a good chap.

Clown
Believe me, thou talkest of an admirable conceited

*Believe me, we're talking about a wonderfully
ingenious*

fellow. Has he any unbraided wares?

fellow. Has he any new goods for sale?

Servant
He hath ribbons of an the colours i' the rainbow;
points more than all the lawyers in Bohemia can
learnedly handle, though they come to him by the
gross: inkles, caddisses, cambrics, lawns: why, he
sings 'em over as they were gods or goddesses; you

*He has ribbons in all the colours of the rainbow;
more laces than all the lawyers in Bohemia could
untangle, even if they came to him in mobs:
linen tapes, garter tapes, cambric, lawn: why he
advertises them as if they were gods or goddesses;
you*

would think a smock were a she-angel, he so chants

*would think that the smock was a female angel, to
hear him sing*

to the sleeve-hand and the work about the square on't.

about its cuffs and the embroidery on the bodice.

Clown
Prithee bring him in; and let him approach singing.

Please bring him in; and let him come in singing.

PERDITA

Forewarn him that he use no scurrilous words in 's tunes.

Exit Servant

Warn him that he is to use no vulgar words in his tunes.

Clown

You have of these pedlars, that have more in them than you'ld think, sister.

There is more to some of these pedlars than you would imagine, sister.

PERDITA

Ay, good brother, or go about to think.

Yes, good brother, more than I want to think about.

Enter AUTOLYCUS, singing

AUTOLYCUS

Lawn as white as driven snow;
Cyprus black as e'er was crow;
Gloves as sweet as damask roses;
Masks for faces and for noses;
Bugle bracelet, necklace amber,
Perfume for a lady's chamber;
Golden quoifs and stomachers,
For my lads to give their dears:
Pins and poking-sticks of steel,
What maids lack from head to heel:
Come buy of me, come; come buy, come buy;

Buy lads, or else your lasses cry: Come buy.

Lawn as white as driven snow;
crêpe as black as the crow ever was;
gloves as sweet as damask roses;
masks for faces and for noses;
black glass beads strung together, amber necklaces,
perfume for a lady's bedroom;
golden caps and belts,
for the lads to give their sweethearts:
pins and collar stiffeners of steel,
everything a girl could want:
come and buy from me, come! Come and buy! Come and buy!
Buy, lads, don't make your lasses cry.
Come and buy!

Clown

If I were not in love with Mopsa, thou shouldst take no money of me; but being enthralled as I am, it will also be the bondage of certain ribbons and gloves.

If I were not in love with Mopsa, you would get no money from me; but being besotted as I am, I will get you to parcel up some ribbons and gloves.

MOPSA

I was promised them against the feast; but they come not too late now.

I was promised them in time for the feast; but now is not too late.

DORCAS

He hath promised you more than that, or there be liars.

He promised you more than that, or someone is lying.

MOPSA

He hath paid you all he promised you; may be, he has
paid you more, which will shame you to give him

*He has paid you all he promised you; maybe he has
overpaid you, and you're worried you'll have to give*

again.

Clown
Is there no manners left among maids? will they wear their plackets where they should bear their faces? Is there not milking-time, when you are

going to bed, or kiln-hole, to whistle off these

secrets, but you must be tittle-tattling before all

our guests? 'tis well they are whispering: clamour your tongues, and not a word more.

MOPSA
I have done. Come, you promised me a tawdry-lace

and a pair of sweet gloves.

Clown
Have I not told thee how I was cozened by the way and lost all my money?

AUTOLYCUS
And indeed, sir, there are cozeners abroad; therefore it behoves men to be wary.

Clown
Fear not thou, man, thou shalt lose nothing here.

AUTOLYCUS
I hope so, sir; for I have about me many parcels of charge.

Clown
What hast here? ballads?

MOPSA
Pray now, buy some: I love a ballad in print o' life, for then we are sure they are true.

AUTOLYCUS
Here's one to a very doleful tune, how a usurer's

wife was brought to bed of twenty money-bags at a burthen and how she longed to eat adders' heads and toads carbonadoed.

it back.

Don't girls have any manners any more? Will they show their privates where their faces should be? Don't you have milking time, or when you're going to bed,
or sitting round the oven, to whisper about these secrets?
Do you have to gossip about it in front of all our guests?

I've finished. Come on, you promised me a coloured scarf
and a pair of scented gloves.

Didn't I tell you how I was conned on the road and lost all my money?

Indeed, sir, there are conmen around; everyone should be careful.

Don't you worry, man, you won't lose anything here.

I hope not, sir; I have many valuable items with me.

What's this you've got? Ballads?

Now please, buy some: I love a printed ballad, I swear, because then we know we've got the right words.

Here's one, which has a very sad tune, about a moneylender's
wife who was pregnant with twenty moneybags, and how she wanted to eat adders' heads and fried toads.

MOPSA
Is it true, think you?

Is it true, do you think?

AUTOLYCUS
Very true, and but a month old.

Very true, and just a month old.

DORCAS
Bless me from marrying a usurer!

Save me from marrying a money lender!

AUTOLYCUS
Here's the midwife's name to't, one Mistress
Tale-porter, and five or six honest wives that were

present. Why should I carry lies abroad?

*You can see it's signed by the midwife, one Mistress
Tale-Porter, as well as five or six honest women that
were
there. Why would I broadcast lies?*

MOPSA
Pray you now, buy it.

Please, buy it.

Clown
Come on, lay it by: and let's first see moe
ballads; we'll buy the other things anon.

*Come on, put it on one side: let's see more
ballads first; we'll buy the other things in due
course.*

AUTOLYCUS
Here's another ballad of a fish, that appeared upon
the coast on Wednesday the four-score of April,
forty thousand fathom above water, and sung this
ballad against the hard hearts of maids: it was
thought she was a woman and was turned into a cold

fish for she would not exchange flesh with one that
loved her: the ballad is very pitiful and as true.

*Here's another ballad about a fish, that appeared
off the coast on Wednesday the 80th of April,
forty thousand fathoms out of the water, and sang
this ballad against the hard hearts of maids:
it was thought she was a woman and was turned
into a cold
fish because she would not give her body to someone
who loved her: the ballot is as sad as it is true.*

DORCAS
Is it true too, think you?

You think it is true as well?

AUTOLYCUS
Five justices' hands at it, and witnesses more than
my pack will hold.

*Five judges have signed to it, and more witnesses
then I could fit in my pack.*

Clown
Lay it by too: another.

Put that to one side too: tell us about another.

AUTOLYCUS
This is a merry ballad, but a very pretty one.

This is a jolly ballad, but a very pretty one.

MOPSA
Let's have some merry ones.

Let's have some jolly ones.

AUTOLYCUS
Why, this is a passing merry one and goes to the tune of 'Two maids wooing a man:' there's scarce a maid westward but she sings it; 'tis in request, I can tell you.

Well, this is a very jolly one and goes to the tune of 'Two maids wooing a man:' all the girls to the west of here are singing it; it's very much the fashion, I can tell you.

MOPSA
We can both sing it: if thou'lt bear a part, thou shalt hear; 'tis in three parts.

We can both sing it: if you take a part, you will hear it; it is in three parts.

DORCAS
We had the tune on't a month ago.

The tune of it got here a month ago.

AUTOLYCUS
I can bear my part; you must know 'tis my occupation; have at it with you.

I can sing my part; you know this is my job; let's all sing together.

SONG

AUTOLYCUS
Get you hence, for I must go
Where it fits not you to know.

*Go away, for I must go
to a place you cannot know of.*

DORCAS
Whither?

Where?

MOPSA
O, whither?

Oh, where?

DORCAS
Whither?

Where?

MOPSA
It becomes thy oath full well,
Thou to me thy secrets tell.

*You should keep your promise,
and tell me all your secrets.*

DORCAS
Me too, let me go thither.

Me too, let me go there.

MOPSA
Or thou goest to the grange or mill.

Or you're going to the farm or the mill.

DORCAS
If to either, thou dost ill.

If to either, you're doing wrong.

AUTOLYCUS

Neither.

DORCAS
What, neither?

AUTOLYCUS
Neither.

DORCAS
Thou hast sworn my love to be.

MOPSA
Thou hast sworn it more to me:
Then whither goest? say, whither?

Clown
We'll have this song out anon by ourselves: my
father and the gentlemen are in sad talk, and we'll

not trouble them. Come, bring away thy pack after

me. Wenches, I'll buy for you both. Pedlar, let's
have the first choice. Follow me, girls.

Exit with DORCAS and MOPSA

AUTOLYCUS
And you shall pay well for 'em.

Follows singing

Will you buy any tape,
Or lace for your cape,
My dainty duck, my dear-a?
Any silk, any thread,
Any toys for your head,
Of the new'st and finest, finest wear-a?
Come to the pedlar;
Money's a medler.
That doth utter all men's ware-a.

Exit

Re-enter Servant

Servant
Master, there is three carters, three shepherds,
three neat-herds, three swine-herds, that have made

Neither.

What, neither?

Neither.

You have sworn to be my love.

*You swore it more to me:
so where are you going? Tell me, where?*

*We'll sing this song between ourselves soon: my
father and the gentlemen are talking seriously, and
we'll
leave them to it. Come with me and bring your
goods.
Girls, I'll treat you both. Pedlar, give us
first choice. Follow me, girls.*

And you will pay well for them.

*Will you buy any tape,
or lace for your cape,
my sweet duck, my dear?
Any silk, any thread,
any decorations for your head,
of the newest and finest style?
Come to the pedlar;
money gets involved
when men are offering their goods.*

*Master, there are three carters, three shepherds,
three cowherds, three swine-herds, that have dress*

themselves all men of hair, they call themselves
Saltiers, and they have a dance which the wenches
say is a gallimaufry of gambols, because they are
not in't; but they themselves are o' the mind, if it
be not too rough for some that know little but
bowling, it will please plentifully.

themselves
up in skins, they call themselves
Saltiers, and they have a dance which the girls
say is a mess, because they are
not in it; but they would like to please you with it
if it's not too rough for those who don't do anything
more exciting than a game of bowls.

Shepherd
Away! we'll none on 't: here has been too much
homely foolery already. I know, sir, we weary you.

Go away! We won't have it: there has been too much
vulgar tomfoolery already. I know, sir, we are tiring
you.

POLIXENES
You weary those that refresh us: pray, let's see
these four threes of herdsmen.

You're only tiring the ones that are entertaining us:
please, let's have a look at these four trios of
herdsmen.

Servant
One three of them, by their own report, sir, hath
danced before the king; and not the worst of the
three but jumps twelve foot and a half by the squier.

One of the trios, according to them, sir, has
danced for the king; and the best one
of the three can jump exactly twelve and a half feet.

Shepherd
Leave your prating: since these good men are
pleased, let them come in; but quickly now.

Quit your jabbering: since these good men have
agreed, let them come in; look sharp about it.

Servant
Why, they stay at door, sir.

Why, they're just at the door, sir.

Exit

*

Here a dance of twelve Satyrs

Here is a dance of twelve satyrs.

POLIXENES
O, father, you'll know more of that hereafter.

Oh, father, you'll know more about that later.

To CAMILLO

Is it not too far gone? 'Tis time to part them.

Hasn't this gone far enough? It's time to separate
them.

He's simple and tells much.

He's simple and has told us plenty.

To FLORIZEL

How now, fair shepherd!
Your heart is full of something that does take
Your mind from feasting. Sooth, when I was young

Hello there, fair shepherd!
Your heart is full of something that takes
your mind off the feast. I swear, when I was young

And handed love as you do, I was wont
To load my she with knacks: I would have ransack'd
The pedlar's silken treasury and have pour'd it
To her acceptance; you have let him go
And nothing marted with him. If your lass
Interpretation should abuse and call this
Your lack of love or bounty, you were straited
For a reply, at least if you make a care
Of happy holding her.

FLORIZEL
Old sir, I know
She prizes not such trifles as these are:
The gifts she looks from me are pack'd and lock'd
Up in my heart; which I have given already,
But not deliver'd. O, hear me breathe my life
Before this ancient sir, who, it should seem,
Hath sometime loved! I take thy hand, this hand,

As soft as dove's down and as white as it,
Or Ethiopian's tooth, or the fann'd
snow that's bolted
By the northern blasts twice o'er.

POLIXENES
What follows this?
How prettily the young swain seems to wash
The hand was fair before! I have put you out:
But to your protestation; let me hear
What you profess.

FLORIZEL
Do, and be witness to 't.

POLIXENES
And this my neighbour too?

FLORIZEL
And he, and more
Than he, and men, the earth, the heavens, and all:
That, were I crown'd the most imperial monarch,

Thereof most worthy, were I the fairest youth

That ever made eye swerve, had force and
knowledge
More than was ever man's, I would not prize them
Without her love; for her employ them all;

*and fell in love as you have, I used
to load my girl with gifts: I would have stripped
the pedlar's silken treasury and offered
it all to her; you have let him go
without doing a single deal. If your girl
takes this the wrong way, and accuses you
of a lack of love or generosity, you would be
hard-pressed for a reply, at least if you care
about making her happy.*

*Old gentleman, I know
she doesn't care about these fripperies:
the gifts she wants from me are packed and locked
up in my heart, which I have given already,
but not delivered. Let me make my vows of love
before this ancient gentleman, who, it would seem,
was once a lover himself. I take your hand, this
hand,
as soft as a dove's feathers and as white as them,
or as an Ethiopian's tooth, or the blown snow
that's been twice sifted by the north wind.*

*What's all this?
How much nicer the young lad seems to make
the hand that was lovely already! I have upset you:
but on to your protestation; let me hear
what you have to say.*

Do, and you can witness it.

And my neighbour here too?

*Him too, and more
than him, and men, the Earth, the heavens, and all:
so that, if I were crowned the most powerful
monarch,
and fully deserved it, if I was the most handsome
youth
that ever caught the eye, had greater strength and
knowledge
than any man ever had, I would not value them
without her love; I would use them all for her;*

Commend them and condemn them to her service
Or to their own perdition.

*I would offer them to her service or else
get rid of them.*

POLIXENES
Fairly offer'd.

A good offer.

CAMILLO
This shows a sound affection.

This shows a true love.

Shepherd
But, my daughter,
Say you the like to him?

*But, my daughter,
do you feel the same way?*

PERDITA
I cannot speak
So well, nothing so well; no, nor mean better:
By the pattern of mine own thoughts I cut out
The purity of his.

*I cannot speak
as well, nothing so good; nor could I mean better:
I shape my thoughts exactly
to the mould of his.*

Shepherd
Take hands, a bargain!
And, friends unknown, you shall bear witness to 't:
I give my daughter to him, and will make
Her portion equal his.

*Join your hands, it's a deal!
And, unknown friends, you will witness it:
I give my daughter to him, and will give her
a dowry to match his fortune.*

FLORIZEL
O, that must be
I' the virtue of your daughter: one being dead,

I shall have more than you can dream of yet;
Enough then for your wonder. But, come on,
Contract us 'fore these witnesses.

*Oh, the fortune must be
the virtues of your daughter: when one person is
dead,
I shall have more than you can ever dream of;
but let's wait until that happens. But, come on,
join us in front of these witnesses.*

Shepherd
Come, your hand;
And, daughter, yours.

*Come, give me your hand;
and, daughter, yours.*

POLIXENES
Soft, swain, awhile, beseech you;
Have you a father?

*Please, lad, just a moment;
do you have a father?*

FLORIZEL
I have: but what of him?

I have: but what about him?

POLIXENES
Knows he of this?

Does he know about this?

FLORIZEL
He neither does nor shall.

He doesn't and he won't.

POLIXENES
Methinks a father
Is at the nuptial of his son a guest
That best becomes the table. Pray you once more,
Is not your father grown incapable
Of reasonable affairs? is he not stupid
With age and altering rheums? can he speak? hear?

I think a father
is the most important guest
at his son's wedding. Let me ask you,
has your father become incapable
of behaving normally? Has he become
senile with age and changing health? Can he speak?
Hear?

Know man from man? dispute his own estate?

Distinguish one man from another? Run his own
household?

Lies he not bed-rid? and again does nothing
But what he did being childish?

Is he bedridden? Can he do nothing
but the things he did as a child?

FLORIZEL
No, good sir;
He has his health and ampler strength indeed
Than most have of his age.

No, good sir;
he has his health, and is in fact stronger
than most men of his age.

POLIXENES
By my white beard,
You offer him, if this be so, a wrong
Something unfilial: reason my son
Should choose himself a wife, but as good reason
The father, all whose joy is nothing else
But fair posterity, should hold some counsel
In such a business.

By my white beard,
if that's the case you are doing him a wrong
that a son should not: it is permissible
for a son to choose himself a wife, but just as much
the father, whose happiness is all to do with
his descendants, should have some say
in the matter.

FLORIZEL
I yield all this;
But for some other reasons, my grave sir,
Which 'tis not fit you know, I not acquaint
My father of this business.

I agree with everything you say;
but there are some other reasons, respected sir,
which I can't tell you about, for not telling
my father about this business.

POLIXENES
Let him know't.

Let him know about it.

FLORIZEL
He shall not.

He will not.

POLIXENES
Prithee, let him.

Please, let him.

FLORIZEL
No, he must not.

No, he must not know.

Shepherd
Let him, my son: he shall not need to grieve
At knowing of thy choice.

*Let him know, my son: he'll have no reason
to object to your choice.*

FLORIZEL
Come, come, he must not.
Mark our contract.

*I'm telling you, he must not know.
Make the contract.*

POLIXENES
Mark your divorce, young sir,

Make a divorce, young sir,

Discovering himself

[taking off his disguise]

Whom son I dare not call; thou art too base
To be acknowledged: thou a sceptre's heir,
That thus affect'st a sheep-hook! Thou old traitor,

*whom I dare not call my son; you are too low
to be acknowledged: you, heir to a kingdom,
dressed up as a shepherd! As for you, you old
traitor,*

I am sorry that by hanging thee I can
But shorten thy life one week. And thou, fresh piece
Of excellent witchcraft, who of force must know
The royal fool thou copest with,--

*I'm sorry that by hanging you I can
only shorten your life by week. And you, young
witch, who must certainly know
what a royal fool you're involved with—*

Shepherd
O, my heart!

Oh, my heart!

POLIXENES
I'll have thy beauty scratch'd with briers, and made
More homely than thy state. For thee, fond boy,

*I'll have your beauty torn with brambles, and made
even more unattractive than your position. As for
you, stupid boy,*

If I may ever know thou dost but sigh
That thou no more shalt see this knack, as never
I mean thou shalt, we'll bar thee from succession;

*if I ever hear that you utter a single sigh
because you will never again see this slut, as
I intend you never shall, I'll strip you of your
inheritance;*

Not hold thee of our blood, no, not our kin,
Far than Deucalion off: mark thou my words:
Follow us to the court. Thou churl, for this time,

*you would no longer be of my blood, no, no relation,
further off than Noah: you mark my words!
Follow me to the court. You, peasant, for the
moment,*

Though full of our displeasure, yet we free thee

*though you have incurred my displeasure, I'll excuse
you*

From the dead blow of it. And you, enchantment.--
Worthy enough a herdsman: yea, him too,
That makes himself, but for our honour therein,

*from its mortal blow. And you, you witch—
good enough for a shepherd; yes, for him too,
who has put himself so low down that if it wasn't for
my royal blood*

Unworthy thee,--if ever henceforth thou
These rural latches to his entrance open,

*he would be beneath you. If you ever
open your door to him again, or take him in your
arms,*

Or hoop his body more with thy embraces,
I will devise a death as cruel for thee

*I shall invent as cruel a method of execution for you
as you can stand.*

As thou art tender to't.

Exit

PERDITA
Even here undone
I was not much afeard; for once or twice
I was about to speak and tell him plainly,
The selfsame sun that shines upon his court
Hides not his visage from our cottage but
Looks on alike. Will't please you, sir, be gone?

I told you what would come of this: beseech you,
Of your own state take care: this dream of mine,--
Being now awake, I'll queen it no inch farther,

But milk my ewes and weep.

Even in this downfall
I was not very frightened; once or twice
I was about to speak and tell him straight
that the same sun that shines on his court
does not hide its face from our cottage
that shines down just the same. Will you please go,
sir?
I told you that this would happen: please
look after yourself: this dream I had--
now I'm awake, I shan't step an inch closer to being
a queen,
I shall just milk my ewes, and weep.

CAMILLO
Why, how now, father!
Speak ere thou diest.

What's to do, father!
Speak before you die.

Shepherd
I cannot speak, nor think
Nor dare to know that which I know. O sir!
You have undone a man of fourscore three,
That thought to fill his grave in quiet, yea,
To die upon the bed my father died,
To lie close by his honest bones: but now
Some hangman must put on my shroud and lay me
Where no priest shovels in dust. O cursed wretch,
That knew'st this was the prince,
and wouldst adventure
To mingle faith with him! Undone! undone!
If I might die within this hour, I have lived
To die when I desire.

I cannot speak, nor think,
or dare to know the things I know. O sir!
You have brought down a man of eighty-three,
that thought he was headed for a peaceful grave;
to die on the bed my father died on,
to be buried next to his honest bones: but now
some hangman will prepare my corpse and bury me
in the unhallowed ground. O you cursed wretch,
who knew this was the prince, and still tried
to have a relationship with him! This is the end!
If I can die within the hour, I have lived
as long as I want to.

Exit

FLORIZEL
Why look you so upon me?
I am but sorry, not afeard; delay'd,
But nothing alter'd: what I was, I am;
More straining on for plucking back, not following
My leash unwillingly.

Why'd you look at me like this?
I am sorry, but not afraid; delayed,
but not blocked: I'm still the same person;
this setback makes me more keen to proceed,
I don't need any persuading.

CAMILLO
Gracious my lord,

My gracious lord,

You know your father's temper: at this time

He will allow no speech, which I do guess
You do not purpose to him; and as hardly
Will he endure your sight as yet, I fear:
Then, till the fury of his highness settle,
Come not before him.

FLORIZEL
I not purpose it.
I think, Camillo?

CAMILLO
Even he, my lord.

PERDITA
How often have I told you 'twould be thus!
How often said, my dignity would last
But till 'twere known!

FLORIZEL
It cannot fail but by
The violation of my faith; and then
Let nature crush the sides o' the earth together
And mar the seeds within! Lift up thy looks:
From my succession wipe me, father; I
Am heir to my affection.

CAMILLO
Be advised.

FLORIZEL
I am, and by my fancy: if my reason
Will thereto be obedient, I have reason;
If not, my senses, better pleased with madness,
Do bid it welcome.

CAMILLO
This is desperate, sir.

FLORIZEL
So call it: but it does fulfil my vow;

I needs must think it honesty. Camillo,
Not for Bohemia, nor the pomp that may
Be thereat glean'd, for all the sun sees or

you know what your father's temper is like: at the moment
he won't let anyone talk to him, which I assume
you won't try; for now I fear
he would hardly put up with the sight of you:
so, until the anger of his Highness has abated,
don't see him.

I don't intend to.
I think—Camillo?

I am he, my lord.

How often have I told you it would turn out this way!
How often did I say I could only keep my position
until it was known!

You can't lose it unless
I go against my promise; if that happens
let nature crush the sides of the earth together
and destroy all life within! Lift up your face:
father, you can wipe me from the succession; I
will inherit my love.

Be warned.

I am, by my emotions: if my reason
obeys them, I have reason;
if not, my senses, preferring madness,
welcomes it.

This is terrible, sir.

You can call it that: but all it does is keep my promise;
so I shall call it honesty. Camillo,
not for the throne of Bohemia, nor the glory
that can be gained from it, not for all the sun shines on,

96

The close earth wombs or the profound sea hides
In unknown fathoms, will I break my oath
To this my fair beloved: therefore, I pray you,
As you have ever been my father's honour'd friend,

When he shall miss me,--as, in faith, I mean not
To see him any more,--cast your good counsels
Upon his passion; let myself and fortune
Tug for the time to come. This you may know
And so deliver, I am put to sea
With her whom here I cannot hold on shore;
And most opportune to our need I have
A vessel rides fast by, but not prepared
For this design. What course I mean to hold
Shall nothing benefit your knowledge, nor
Concern me the reporting.

CAMILLO
O my lord!
I would your spirit were easier for advice,
Or stronger for your need.

FLORIZEL
Hark, Perdita

Drawing her aside

I'll hear you by and by.

CAMILLO
He's irremoveable,
Resolved for flight. Now were I happy, if
His going I could frame to serve my turn,
Save him from danger, do him love and honour,
Purchase the sight again of dear Sicilia
And that unhappy king, my master, whom
I so much thirst to see.

FLORIZEL
Now, good Camillo;
I am so fraught with curious business that
I leave out ceremony.

CAMILLO
Sir, I think
You have heard of my poor services, i' the love

or that is hidden in the earth, or the deep sea hides
in its unknown depths, will I break my oath
to my beautiful love here. So, I ask you,
as you have always been my father's honoured
friend,
when he misses me—as, I swear, I intend
never to see him again—add your good advice
to his anger: as for the future,
I shall take my chances. You can know this,
and tell him, that I have gone to sea
with the one whom I cannot stay with on shore;
and luckily for us, I have
a ship at anchor nearby, though not meant
for this plan. The direction I mean to take
it will do you no good to know, so I won't
bother telling you.

Oh my lord!
I wish your spirit was more open to advice,
or more aware that you need it.

Listen, Perdita.

[to Camillo] I'll listen to you in a while.

His mind is made up,
he's decided to flee. Now I would be happy, if
I could use his departure to serve my own plans,
save him from danger, give him love and honour,
and get to see dear Sicily again,
and that unhappy king, my master, whom
I want to see so much.

Now, good Camillo;
I am so full of anxious business that
I've forgotten my manners.

Sir, I think
you have heard of my poor services, done for the
love

That I have borne your father?

of your father?

FLORIZEL
Very nobly
Have you deserved: it is my father's music
To speak your deeds, not little of his care
To have them recompensed as thought on.

You have
acquitted yourself very nobly: my father loves
to talk of what you have done, and is always thinking
about how you can be rewarded.

CAMILLO
Well, my lord,
If you may please to think I love the king
And through him what is nearest to him, which is
Your gracious self, embrace but my direction:
If your more ponderous and settled project
May suffer alteration, on mine honour,
I'll point you where you shall have such receiving
As shall become your highness; where you may
Enjoy your mistress, from the whom, I see,
There's no disjunction to be made, but by--
As heavens forefend!--your ruin; marry her,
And, with my best endeavours in your absence,
Your discontenting father strive to qualify
And bring him up to liking.

Well, my lord,
if you believe that I love the king,
and by association what is nearest to him, which is
your gracious self, take my advice,
if your more important and determined plan
can accommodate some alteration. I promise you
I shall direct you to where you will get a welcome
befitting your highness; where you may
enjoy your mistress; for I can see
that the only thing that would split you up would be–
may heaven forbid it!–Your death. Marry her,
and while you are away I shall do my best
to pacify your unhappy father,
and bring him round.

FLORIZEL
How, Camillo,
May this, almost a miracle, be done?
That I may call thee something more than man
And after that trust to thee.

How, Camillo,
can this almost miracle be done?
If it is I'll call you a superman
and always trust you.

CAMILLO
Have you thought on
A place whereto you'll go?

Have you thought about
where you will go?

FLORIZEL
Not any yet:
But as the unthought-on accident is guilty
To what we wildly do, so we profess
Ourselves to be the slaves of chance and flies
Of every wind that blows.

I haven't yet:
since the unexpected misfortune is what
prompts us to rush away, so I admit
we are the slaves of chance and must go
wherever the wind takes us.

CAMILLO
Then list to me:
This follows, if you will not change your purpose

Then listen to me:
this is what you should do, if you won't change your
mind

But undergo this flight, make for Sicilia,

and still wish to flee, make for Sicily,

And there present yourself and your fair princess,
For so I see she must be, 'fore Leontes:
She shall be habited as it becomes
The partner of your bed. Methinks I see
Leontes opening his free arms and weeping
His welcomes forth; asks thee the son forgiveness,
As 'twere i' the father's person; kisses the hands

Of your fresh princess; o'er and o'er divides him
'Twixt his unkindness and his kindness; the one
He chides to hell and bids the other grow
Faster than thought or time.

FLORIZEL
Worthy Camillo,
What colour for my visitation shall I
Hold up before him?

CAMILLO
Sent by the king your father
To greet him and to give him comforts. Sir,

The manner of your bearing towards him, with
What you as from your father shall deliver,
Things known betwixt us three, I'll write you down:

The which shall point you forth at every sitting
What you must say; that he shall not perceive
But that you have your father's bosom there
And speak his very heart.

FLORIZEL
I am bound to you:
There is some sap in this.

CAMILLO
A cause more promising
Than a wild dedication of yourselves
To unpath'd waters, undream'd shores, most certain
To miseries enough; no hope to help you,
But as you shake off one to take another;
Nothing so certain as your anchors, who
Do their best office, if they can but stay you
Where you'll be loath to be: besides you know
Prosperity's the very bond of love,
Whose fresh complexion and whose heart together
Affliction alters.

and there present yourself and your fair princess,
for I see that's what she must be, to Leontes:
she shall be welcomed as is fitting
for your partner. I can imagine
Leontes opening his generous arms and weeping
out his welcome; he'll ask you, the son,
to forgive him in the name of the father; he'll kiss the hands
of your young princess; he'll talk alternately
of his unkindness and his kindness, damning
one to hell, and telling the other to grow
faster than thought or time.

Good Camillo,
what reason should I give him
for my visit?

Say you have been sent by the king your father
to greet him and to give him assurances of
friendship. Sir,
the way you should behave towards him, and
what you shall deliver as if it came from your father,
things only known to the three of us, I'll write down
for you:
this will tell you in every situation
what you should say, so he will believe
that you have all your father's confidence
and speak his heart to you.

I'm obliged to you:
this is a wise plan.

A plan more promising
than wildly throwing yourselves
into unmapped waters, unknown shores, certain
to bring you hardships; with no hope for you
as one follows after another;
the most certain thing would be your anchor, which
at best can only keep you
where you don't want to be: anyway you know
prosperity is the sealant of love,
whose charming looks and whose heart
can be changed by hardship.

PERDITA

One of these is true:
I think affliction may subdue the cheek,
But not take in the mind.

One of those things is true:
I think hardship might change the looks,
but it won't change the mind.

CAMILLO

Yea, say you so?
There shall not at your father's house these
seven years
Be born another such.

Is that what you say?
There won't be another like you
born at your father's house
for an age.

FLORIZEL

My good Camillo,
She is as forward of her breeding as
She is i' the rear our birth.

My good Camillo,
she is as high in nobility as
she is low in birth.

CAMILLO

I cannot say 'tis pity
She lacks instructions, for she seems a mistress

To most that teach.

I can't say that it's a shame
that she hasn't been educated, for she seems
superior
to most teachers.

PERDITA

Your pardon, sir; for this
I'll blush you thanks.

You'll excuse me, sir; for this
I'll show my thanks with a blush.

FLORIZEL

My prettiest Perdita!
But O, the thorns we stand upon! Camillo,
Preserver of my father, now of me,
The medicine of our house, how shall we do?
We are not furnish'd like Bohemia's son,
Nor shall appear in Sicilia.

My prettiest Perdita!
But oh, I feel like I'm on hot bricks! Camillo,
saviour of my father, now of me,
the doctor of our house, what shall we do?
I'm not dressed like Bohemia's son,
and I won't seem so in Sicily.

CAMILLO

My lord,
Fear none of this: I think you know my fortunes
Do all lie there: it shall be so my care
To have you royally appointed as if
The scene you play were mine. For instance, sir,
That you may know you shall not want, one word.

My lord,
don't worry about that: I think you know my fortune
is still all there: I will make it my business
to have you so royally dressed as if
I was directing your scene for you. For instance, sir,
so you know you won't lack for anything, let's have a
word.

They talk aside

Re-enter AUTOLYCUS

AUTOLYCUS

Ha, ha! what a fool Honesty is! and Trust, his
sworn brother, a very simple gentleman! I have sold
all my trumpery; not a counterfeit stone, not a
ribbon, glass, pomander, brooch, table-book, ballad,
knife, tape, glove, shoe-tie, bracelet, horn-ring,
to keep my pack from fasting: they throng who
should buy first, as if my trinkets had been

hallowed and brought a benediction to the buyer:
by which means I saw whose purse was best in
picture; and what I saw, to my good use I

remembered. My clown, who wants but something to
be a reasonable man, grew so in love with the
wenches' song, that he would not stir his pettitoes
till he had both tune and words; which so drew the

rest of the herd to me that all their other senses

stuck in ears: you might have pinched a placket, it
was senseless; 'twas nothing to geld a codpiece of a

purse; I could have filed keys off that hung in

chains: no hearing, no feeling, but my sir's song,

and admiring the nothing of it. So that in this
time of lethargy I picked and cut most of their
festival purses; and had not the old man come in

with a whoo-bub against his daughter and the king's
son and scared my choughs from the chaff, I had not

left a purse alive in the whole army.

CAMILLO, FLORIZEL, and PERDITA come forward

CAMILLO

Nay, but my letters, by this means being there
So soon as you arrive, shall clear that doubt.

FLORIZEL

And those that you'll procure from King Leontes--

CAMILLO

Shall satisfy your father.

*Ha ha! How stupid Honesty is! And Trust, his
sworn brother, is a very simple gentleman! I have
sold all my rubbish: not a fake stone, not a
ribbon, glass, pomander, brooch, notebook,
ballad, knife, tape, gloves, shoelace, bracelet,
magic ring is left in my empty pack: they mobbed
me for the privilege of buying first, as if my trinkets
were
sacred and gave a blessing to the buyer:
because of that I saw whose purse was best for
pinching, and what I saw I remembered for my
benefit.
My clown (who's not really all there)
became so in love with the girls singing,
that he would not move his trotters until he had both
the tune and the words; that pulled the rest of the
herd
so close to me, that only their ears were working:
you
might have pinched a bodice, they were so oblivious;
it was nothing to cut a purse away from a trouser
pocket; I could
have filed off the keys that hung from chains: they
heard nothing,
felt nothing, but my lad's song, admiring its
worthlessness.
So in this quiet interval I picked and cut
most of their dress purses; and if
the old man hadn't come in making a hullabaloo
about his
daughter and the king's son, and scared the birds
away from the bait, not one of those purses would
have survived.*

*It's all right, my letters, through being there
as soon as you arrive, will stop that doubt.*

And those that you'll get from King Leontes–

Will please your father.

101

PERDITA
Happy be you!
All that you speak shows fair.

Blessings upon you!
Everything you say is good.

CAMILLO
Who have we here?

Who have we here?

Seeing AUTOLYCUS

We'll make an instrument of this, omit
Nothing may give us aid.

We'll use this as a tool, we shan't
neglect anything that could help us.

AUTOLYCUS
If they have overheard me now, why, hanging.

If they overheard what I said just now, I'll be hung.

CAMILLO
How now, good fellow! why shakest thou so? Fear

not, man; here's no harm intended to thee.

Hello there, good fellow! Why are you shaking?
Don't
be afraid, man; we don't mean you any harm.

AUTOLYCUS
I am a poor fellow, sir.

I am a poor man, sir.

CAMILLO
Why, be so still; here's nobody will steal that from

thee: yet for the outside of thy poverty we must

make an exchange; therefore discase thee instantly,
--thou must think there's a necessity in't,--and
change garments with this gentleman: though the

pennyworth on his side be the worst, yet hold thee,
there's some boot.

Well, you can carry on being one; there's nobody
here who will
steal that away from you: but we want to make a
swap
for your poor appearance; undress yourself at once—
you must believe this is essential—and
swap clothes with this gentleman: although he's
getting
the rough end of the bargain, if you wait
there will be some reward.

AUTOLYCUS
I am a poor fellow, sir.

I am a poor fellow, sir.

Aside

I know ye well enough.

I know who you are well enough.

CAMILLO
Nay, prithee, dispatch: the gentleman is half
flayed already.

Now, please hurry: this gentleman is half
undressed already.

AUTOLYCUS
Are you in earnest, sir?

Are you serious, sir?

Aside

I smell the trick on't.

I can see a trap here.

FLORIZEL
Dispatch, I prithee.

Hurry, please.

AUTOLYCUS
Indeed, I have had earnest: but I cannot with
conscience take it.

*Well, you've paid a deposit: but I can't
in all conscience take it.*

CAMILLO
Unbuckle, unbuckle.

Undress, undress.

FLORIZEL and AUTOLYCUS exchange garments

Fortunate mistress,--let my prophecy
Come home to ye!--you must retire yourself
Into some covert: take your sweetheart's hat
And pluck it o'er your brows, muffle your face,

Dismantle you, and, as you can, disliken
The truth of your own seeming; that you may--
For I do fear eyes over--to shipboard

Get undescried.

*Lucky mistress–may those words
be proved true!–You must go off
into the woods: take your sweetheart's hat
and pull it down over your forehead, wrap up your
face,
undress, and as much as you can disguise
your appearance; so you can–
because I'm worried about spies–get on board the
ship
without being spotted.*

PERDITA
I see the play so lies
That I must bear a part.

*I see the way the play is going,
so that I must take a part.*

CAMILLO
No remedy.
Have you done there?

*It can't be helped.
Are you finished?*

FLORIZEL
Should I now meet my father,
He would not call me son.

*If I met my father now,
he wouldn't recognise me.*

CAMILLO
Nay, you shall have no hat.

No, you will go bareheaded.

Giving it to PERDITA

[gives the hat to Perdita]

Come, lady, come. Farewell, my friend.

Come on, lady, come on. Goodbye, my friend.

AUTOLYCUS
Adieu, sir.

Goodbye, sir.

FLORIZEL
O Perdita, what have we twain forgot!
Pray you, a word.

Oh Perdita, what have we two forgotten!
Please, a word.

CAMILLO
[Aside] What I do next, shall be to tell the king
Of this escape and whither they are bound;
Wherein my hope is I shall so prevail
To force him after: in whose company
I shall review Sicilia, for whose sight

I have a woman's longing.

What I shall do next will be to tell the king
about this escape and where they are going;
and so I hope that I can persuade him
to chase after them: going with him
I shall see Sicily again, which I have been longing
for
like a woman.

FLORIZEL
Fortune speed us!
Thus we set on, Camillo, to the sea-side.

Good luck to us!
So we're setting off, Camillo, to the sea shore.

CAMILLO
The swifter speed the better.

The quicker you go the better.

Exeunt FLORIZEL, PERDITA, and CAMILLO

AUTOLYCUS
I understand the business, I hear it: to have an

open ear, a quick eye, and a nimble hand, is
necessary for a cut-purse; a good nose is requisite
also, to smell out work for the other senses. I see
this is the time that the unjust man doth thrive.
What an exchange had this been without boot! What

a boot is here with this exchange! Sure the gods do

this year connive at us, and we may do any thing
extempore. The prince himself is about a piece of
iniquity, stealing away from his father with his

clog at his heels: if I thought it were a piece of
honesty to acquaint the king withal, I would not

do't: I hold it the more knavery to conceal it;
and therein am I constant to my profession.

I understand what's going on, I've heard it. To have
an open
ear, a quick eye, and a nimble hand, is necessary for
a pickpocket; you also need a good nose, to sniff out
work for the other senses. I can see this is the time
for the criminal type to prosper. What a swap
this would have been without any reward! What a
reward
I got with this swap! It's certain the gods have
decided this is
my year, I don't even need to plan anything.
The prince himself is up to no good
(sneaking away from his father with his ball and
chain):
if I thought it was the honest thing to do
to let the king know about it, I wouldn't do it: I think
it
is more wicked to keep it hidden; and so I stick
to the rules of my profession.

Re-enter Clown and Shepherd

Aside, aside; here is more matter for a hot brain:

every lane's end, every shop, church, session,
hanging, yields a careful man work.

Clown
See, see; what a man you are now!
There is no other way but to tell the king
she's a changeling and none of your flesh and blood.

Shepherd
Nay, but hear me.

Clown
Nay, but hear me.

Shepherd
Go to, then.

Clown
She being none of your flesh and blood, your flesh
and blood has not offended the king; and so your
flesh and blood is not to be punished by him. Show

those things you found about her, those secret
things, all but what she has with her: this being

done, let the law go whistle: I warrant you.

Shepherd
I will tell the king all, every word, yea, and his
son's pranks too; who, I may say, is no honest man,

neither to his father nor to me, to go about to make

me the king's brother-in-law.

Clown
Indeed, brother-in-law was the farthest off you

could have been to him and then your blood had been
the dearer by I know how much an ounce.

*I'll just step to one side; here's more business for a
quick mind:*
*every street corner, every shop, church, trial,
hanging, gives the thinking man opportunities.*

You see: what position you're in now!
The only thing is to tell the king
she's a changeling and no relation of yours.

No, but listen to me.

No, you listen to me.

Go on then.

*If she is not your flesh and blood, your flesh
and blood has not offended the King; and so your
flesh and blood will not be punished by him. Show
him*
*those things you found with her, those secret
things, all except what she's taken with her: when
you've*
done this, the law can't touch you: I promise you.

*I'll tell the king everything, every word, yes, and
what his son's been up to as well; who, I might add,
is not a good man,*
*either to his father or to me, going around trying to
make*
me the king's brother-in-law.

*Indeed, you would have been at least his brother-in-
law,*
*and then your blood would have been worth more,
I can tell you the price per ounce.*

AUTOLYCUS
[Aside] Very wisely, puppies!

Very clever, puppies!

Shepherd
Well, let us to the king: there is that in this
fardel will make him scratch his beard.

*Well, let's go to the king: we've got some
things in this bundle that will make him think.*

AUTOLYCUS
[Aside] I know not what impediment this complaint
may be to the flight of my master.

*I don't know how what they're doing will block
my master's flight.*

Clown
Pray heartily he be at palace.

We must hope he'll be at the palace.

AUTOLYCUS
[Aside] Though I am not naturally honest, I am so

sometimes by chance: let me pocket up my pedlar's
excrement.

*Although I am not naturally honest, I am
occasionally
by accident: let me take off my pedlar's disguise.*

Takes off his false beard

How now, rustics! whither are you bound?

Hello there, peasants! Where are you off to?

Shepherd
To the palace, an it like your worship.

To the palace, if your worship pleases.

AUTOLYCUS
Your affairs there, what, with whom, the condition
of that fardel, the place of your dwelling, your
names, your ages, of what having, breeding, and
any
thing that is fitting to be known, discover.

*Tell me what your business is there, with whom,
what's in that bundle, where you live, your
names, your ages, your parentage, your ancestry,
and any
other thing that can be decently told.*

Clown
We are but plain fellows, sir.

We are just plain folk, sir.

AUTOLYCUS
A lie; you are rough and hairy. Let me have no
lying: it becomes none but tradesmen, and they
often give us soldiers the lie: but we pay them for
it with stamped coin, not stabbing steel; therefore
they do not give us the lie.

*That's a lie; you are rough and hairy. Don't give me
any lies: that's only for tradesmen, and they
often give we soldiers the lie: but we pay them
for it with minted coins, not stabbing swords; and so
they do not 'give' us the lie.*

Clown
Your worship had like to have given us one, if you

*Your worship would have given us a lie, if you
hadn't*

had not taken yourself with the manner.

just corrected yourself.

Shepherd
Are you a courtier, an't like you, sir?

Please, sir, are you a courtier?

AUTOLYCUS
Whether it like me or no, I am a courtier. Seest

thou not the air of the court in these enfoldings?
hath not my gait in it the measure of the court?
receives not thy nose court-odor from me? reflect I
not on thy baseness court-contempt? Thinkest thou,

for that I insinuate, or toaze from thee thy
business, I am therefore no courtier? I am courtier

cap-a-pe; and one that will either push on or pluck

back thy business there: whereupon I command thee to
open thy affair.

Whether it pleases me or not, I am a courtier. Can't you see
the courtly cut of my clothes?
Don't I walk like a courtier?
Don't I smell like a courtier? Don't I
look on your vulgarity with the contempt of court?
Do you think
that just because I'm asking you about your
business that makes me no courtier? I am a courtier
head to foot;
and I will either help or hinder your business at
court:
so I'm telling you to tell me what it is.

Shepherd
My business, sir, is to the king.

My business, sir, is with the king.

AUTOLYCUS
What advocate hast thou to him?

Who do you have to speak for you?

Shepherd
I know not, an't like you.

I don't know, if you please.

Clown
Advocate's the court-word for a pheasant: say you
have none.

Advocate is the court word for a pheasant: say you
haven't any.

Shepherd
None, sir; I have no pheasant, cock nor hen.

None, sir; I have no pheasant, neither cock nor hen.

AUTOLYCUS
How blessed are we that are not simple men!
Yet nature might have made me as these are,
Therefore I will not disdain.

How blessed we are who are not simple!
But nature could have made me like these,
so I won't look down on them.

Clown
This cannot be but a great courtier.

This can only be a great courtier.

Shepherd
His garments are rich, but he wears

He has expensive clothes, but he wears

them not handsomely.

them badly.

Clown
He seems to be the more noble in being fantastical:
a great man, I'll warrant; I know by the picking
on's teeth.

He seems to be more noble in his peculiarities:
I'll bet he's a great man; I can tell by the way
he picks his teeth.

AUTOLYCUS
The fardel there? what's i' the fardel?
Wherefore that box?

The bundle there? What's in the bundle?
Why'd you have that box?

Shepherd
Sir, there lies such secrets in this fardel and box,
which none must know but the king; and which he
shall know within this hour, if I may come to the
speech of him.

Sir, there are such secrets in this bundle and box,
that only the king can know; and which he
shall know of within the hour, if I can get within
speaking distance of him.

AUTOLYCUS
Age, thou hast lost thy labour.

Old man, you've missed your chance.

Shepherd
Why, sir?

Why, sir?

AUTOLYCUS
The king is not at the palace; he is gone aboard a
new ship to purge melancholy and air himself: for,

if thou beest capable of things serious, thou must
know the king is full of grief.

The king is not at the palace; he has gone on board
a new ship to shake off depression and get some air:
for,
if you pay attention to important matters, you must
know the king is full of sadness.

Shepard
So 'tis said, sir; about his son, that should have
married a shepherd's daughter.

That's what I've heard, sir; I've heard about his son,
who was going to marry a shepherd's daughter.

AUTOLYCUS
If that shepherd be not in hand-fast, let him fly:
the curses he shall have, the tortures he shall
feel, will break the back of man, the heart of
monster.

If that shepherd isn't under arrest yet, he should run:
the curses he will get, the tortures he will
feel, will break the back of a man, the heart of a
monster.

Clown
Think you so, sir?

Do you think so, sir?

AUTOLYCUS
Not he alone shall suffer what wit can make heavy
and vengeance bitter; but those that are germane to
him, though removed fifty times, shall all come

Not only he will suffer whatever punishment they
can come up with; those who are close to him,
even if hardly related, will all be given

under the hangman: which though it be great pity, yet it is necessary. An old sheep-whistling rogue, a

ram-tender, to offer to have his daughter come into grace! Some say he shall be stoned; but that death is too soft for him, say I; draw our throne into a sheep-cote! all deaths are too few, the sharpest too easy.

to the hangman: it will be a great shame, but it has to be done. An old sheep keeping scoundrel, a ram tender, offering to make his daughter a royal! Some say he will be stoned; but that death is too soft for him I say; dragging our throne into a sheep pen! There is not enough death or pain to punish him.

Clown
Has the old man e'er a son, sir, do you hear. an't like you, sir?

Has the old man got a son, sir, have you heard, if it pleases you, sir?

AUTOLYCUS
He has a son, who shall be flayed alive; then 'nointed over with honey, set on the head of a wasp's nest; then stand till he be three quarters

He has a son, who will be skinned alive; then spread all over with honey and put on top of a wasps' nest; they'll leave him there until he's three quarters

and a dram dead; then recovered again with aqua-vitae or some other hot infusion; then, raw as he is, and in the hottest day prognostication proclaims, shall be be set against a brick-wall, the sun looking with a southward eye upon him, where he is to behold him with flies blown to death. But what talk we of these traitorly rascals, whose miseries

and a bit dead; then they'll revive him with whiskey or some other hot drink; then, skinned as he is, and on the hottest day the forecast predicts, he shall be put up against a brick wall, south facing with the sun beating down on him, and there he will be eaten to death by maggots. But why are we talking about these traitorous rascals, whose miseries should be smiled at,

are to be smiled at, their offences being so capital? Tell me, for you seem to be honest plain

as they have committed such terrible offences? Tell me (for you

men, what you have to the king: being something gently considered, I'll bring you where he is aboard, tender your persons to his presence, whisper him in your behalfs; and if it be in man besides the king to effect your suits, here is man shall do it.

seem to be honest simple men) what's your business with the king: if it seems reasonable, I'll bring you on board his ship, hand you over to him, speak to him on your behalf; and if it's possible for any man, apart from the king, to get you what you want, I am the man to do it.

Clown
He seems to be of great authority: close with him, give him gold; and though authority be a stubborn bear, yet he is oft led by the nose with gold: show the inside of your purse to the outside of his hand, and no more ado. Remember 'stoned,' and 'flayed alive.'

He seems to be very powerful: make a deal with him, give him gold; although power can be a stubborn beast, it can often be tamed with gold: put what's inside your purse on the outside of his hand, and do it quickly. Remember 'stoned,' and 'skinned alive.'

Shepherd
An't please you, sir, to undertake the business for

us, here is that gold I have: I'll make it as much

If you'd be kind enough, sir, to undertake this business for us, here's the gold I have: I'll give you the same more and leave this young man in pawn till I bring it you.

again
and leave you this young man as a pledge until I bring it for you.

AUTOLYCUS
After I have done what I promised?

After I have done what I promise?

Shepherd
Ay, sir.

Yes, sir.

AUTOLYCUS
Well, give me the moiety. Are you a party in this business?

Well, give me my down payment. Are you involved in this business?

Clown
In some sort, sir: but though my case be a pitiful one, I hope I shall not be flayed out of it.

In a way, sir: but although my skin may be worthless, I hope it won't be stripped off me.

AUTOLYCUS
O, that's the case of the shepherd's son: hang him,

he'll be made an example.

Oh, that's what's going to happen with the shepherd's son: hang him,
they'll make an example of him.

Clown
Comfort, good comfort! We must to the king and show
our strange sights: he must know 'tis none of your

daughter nor my sister; we are gone else. Sir, I

will give you as much as this old man does when the
business is performed, and remain, as he says, your
pawn till it be brought you.

God help us! We must go to the king and show

him these strange things: he must know that she is not your
daughter nor my sister; otherwise we're done for. So, I'll
give you the same as this old man has when the business has been done, and I'll stay, as he says, as his pledge until it's brought to you.

AUTOLYCUS
I will trust you. Walk before toward the sea-side; go on the right hand: I will but look upon the

hedge and follow you.

I will trust you. Walk ahead down to the seashore; go on the right-hand side: I'll just pop behind this hedge
for a moment then I'll follow you.

Clown
We are blest in this man, as I may say, even blest.

We are lucky to have this man, I'm telling you, very lucky.

Shepherd
Let's before as he bids us: he was provided to do

Let's go ahead as he has told us: he was sent to help

us good.

us.

Exeunt Shepherd and Clown

AUTOLYCUS
If I had a mind to be honest, I see Fortune would
not suffer me: she drops booties in my mouth. I am

courted now with a double occasion, gold and a
means
to do the prince my master good; which who
knows how
that may turn back to my advancement? I will bring
these two moles, these blind ones, aboard him: if he

think it fit to shore them again and that the

complaint they have to the king concerns him

nothing, let him call me rogue for being so far
officious; for I am proof against that title and
what shame else belongs to't. To him will I present

them: there may be matter in it.

Exit

If I actually felt like being honest, I see fate
wouldn't let me: she drops loot straight into my lap.
I am
now given two opportunities, gold and a way
to do the prince my master good; who knows how
I can turn this round to my advantage? I will bring
these two moles, these blind ones, to him on board:
if he
thinks the thing to do is to put them back on shore
and that the
complaint they have against the king is none of his
business,
let him call me a scoundrel for being so officious;
I don't care if anyone calls me that or
any other shame which goes with it. I will present
them
to him: there might be something in it for me.

Act 5

111

Scene 1

SCENE I. A room in LEONTES' palace.

Enter LEONTES, CLEOMENES, DION, PAULINA, and Servants

CLEOMENES
Sir, you have done enough, and have perform'd
A saint-like sorrow: no fault could you make,
Which you have not redeem'd; indeed, paid down
More penitence than done trespass: at the last,
Do as the heavens have done, forget your evil;
With them forgive yourself.

Sir, you have done enough, and have done penance
like a saint: there is no wrong you could do
which you have not paid for; indeed, you have done
more penance than the sin required: in the end,
forget your evil as the gods have done;
forgive yourself as they have forgiven you.

LEONTES
Whilst I remember
Her and her virtues, I cannot forget
My blemishes in them, and so still think of
The wrong I did myself; which was so much,
That heirless it hath made my kingdom and
Destroy'd the sweet'st companion that e'er man
Bred his hopes out of.

As long as I can remember
her and her goodness, I cannot forget
my evil in comparison, and so I still think of
the things I did wrong; they were so great,
that it has left my kingdom without an heir and
destroyed the sweetest companion that a man ever
took as his mate.

PAULINA
True, too true, my lord:
If, one by one, you wedded all the world,

Or from the all that are took something good,
To make a perfect woman, she you kill'd
Would be unparallel'd.

True, too true, my lord:
if you married every woman in the world
individually:
or took some element from every good woman,
to make a perfect one, you still wouldn't get a match
for the one you killed.

LEONTES
I think so. Kill'd!
She I kill'd! I did so: but thou strikest me
Sorely, to say I did; it is as bitter
Upon thy tongue as in my thought: now, good now,

Say so but seldom.

I agree. Killed!
I killed her! I did: but you wound me
deeply, to say I did; it's as bitter
to hear you say it as it is for me to think it: in this time,
don't say it often.

CLEOMENES
Not at all, good lady:
You might have spoken a thousand things that would
Have done the time more benefit and graced
Your kindness better.

Don't say it at all, good lady:
there are a thousand things you could have said that would
have been more appropriate for the time and suited
your kindness better.

PAULINA

You are one of those
Would have him wed again.

You're one of the ones
who would like him to marry again.

DION
If you would not so,
You pity not the state, nor the remembrance

If you don't want him to,
you don't care about the country, or the continuation

Of his most sovereign name; consider little
What dangers, by his highness' fail of issue,
May drop upon his kingdom and devour
Incertain lookers on. What were more holy
Than to rejoice the former queen is well?
What holier than, for royalty's repair,
For present comfort and for future good,
To bless the bed of majesty again
With a sweet fellow to't?

of his royal line; think a little about
what dangers, through his highness having no heir,
may fall upon this kingdom, and destroy
those who need guidance. What could be more holy
than to rejoice that the former queen is in heaven?
What is holier than, to repair the royal line,
for current happiness and for good in the future,
to bless the royal bed again
with a sweet companion in it?

PAULINA
There is none worthy,
Respecting her that's gone. Besides, the gods

There is nobody worthy of
filling the place of the one who's gone. Besides, the gods

Will have fulfill'd their secret purposes;
For has not the divine Apollo said,
Is't not the tenor of his oracle,
That King Leontes shall not have an heir
Till his lost child be found? which that it shall,
Is all as monstrous to our human reason
As my Antigonus to break his grave
And come again to me; who, on my life,
Did perish with the infant. 'Tis your counsel
My lord should to the heavens be contrary,
Oppose against their wills.

will have their secret plans carried out;
hasn't the divine Apollo said,
wasn't that the message of his oracle,
that King Leontes will not have an heir
until his lost child is found? And the chances
of that happening are as ridiculous as thinking
that my Antigonus will break out of his grave
and come back to me; and I swear
he died with the child. Your advice is
that my lord should fight against the heavens,
and oppose their orders. [to Leontes] Don't worry about

To LEONTES
Care not for issue;
The crown will find an heir: great Alexander
Left his to the worthiest; so his successor
Was like to be the best.

an heir;
the crown will find one. Great Alexander
left his to the most deserving; so his successor
was likely to be the best choice.

LEONTES
Good Paulina,
Who hast the memory of Hermione,
I know, in honour– O, that ever I
Had squared me to thy counsel! then, even now,
I might have look'd upon my queen's full eyes,
Have taken treasure from her lips--

Good Paulina,
who keeps the memory of Hermione,
I know, in honour–Oh, how I wish
that I had followed your advice! Then, even now,
I might be looking at my queen's great eyes,
taking kisses from her lips–

PAULINA
And left them
More rich for what they yielded.

And leaving them
richer for what they had given.

LEONTES
Thou speak'st truth.
No more such wives; therefore, no wife: one worse,

You're saying the truth.
There is no such wife available; therefore I will have no wife: a worse one,

And better used, would make her sainted spirit
Again possess her corpse, and on this stage,
Were we offenders now, appear soul-vex'd,

treated better, would make her blessed spirit
go back into her body, and on this stage,
if we were to become offenders, she would appear with her soul in torment,

And begin, 'Why to me?'

asking, 'Why do you insult me like this?'

PAULINA
Had she such power,
She had just cause.

If she had the power to do it,
she would have a good reason.

LEONTES
She had; and would incense me
To murder her I married.

She would have; she would incite me
to murder the one I married.

PAULINA
I should so:
Were I the ghost that walk'd, I'ld bid you mark
Her eye, and tell me for what dull part in't
You chose her; then I'ld shriek, that even your ears
Should rift to hear me; and the words that follow'd

I would
if I were the ghost that appeared, I'd tell you to look in her eyes, and tell me what part of her dullness made you choose her; and then I'd shriek, so that your ears would split to hear me; and the words that followed

Should be 'Remember mine.'

would be, 'Remember mine.'

LEONTES
Stars, stars,
And all eyes else dead coals! Fear thou no wife;

They were like stars,
and all other eyes are like dead coals! Don't worry about a wife;

I'll have no wife, Paulina.

I'll have no wife, Paulina.

PAULINA
Will you swear
Never to marry but by my free leave?

Will you swear
that you will never marry except with my permission?

LEONTES
Never, Paulina; so be blest my spirit!

Never, Paulina; I swear to it on my soul's salvation!

PAULINA
Then, good my lords, bear witness to his oath.

Then, my good lords, witness his oath.

CLEOMENES
You tempt him over-much.

You are asking him too much.

PAULINA
Unless another,
As like Hermione as is her picture,
Affront his eye.

Unless another,
absolutely identical to Hermione,
comes to his eye.

CLEOMENES
Good madam,--

Good madam—

PAULINA
I have done.
Yet, if my lord will marry,--if you will, sir,
No remedy, but you will,--give me the office
To choose you a queen: she shall not be so young
As was your former; but she shall be such
As, walk'd your first queen's ghost,
it should take joy
To see her in your arms.

I'm finished.
But, if my lord wants to marry—if you must, sir,
if nothing else will do—give me the task
of choosing your queen: she won't be as young
as your previous one; but she will be such a type
that, if your first queen's ghost walked the earth
it would be happy
to see her in your arms.

LEONTES
My true Paulina,
We shall not marry till thou bid'st us.

My loyal Paulina,
I shall not marry until you tell me.

PAULINA
That
Shall be when your first queen's again in breath;
Never till then.

That
will be when your first queen breathes again;
never until then.

Enter a Gentleman

Gentleman
One that gives out himself Prince Florizel,
Son of Polixenes, with his princess, she
The fairest I have yet beheld, desires access
To your high presence.

Someone who announces himself as Prince Florizel,
son of Polixenes, with his princess, who is
the loveliest woman I have ever seen, wants access
to your royal presence.

LEONTES
What with him? he comes not
Like to his father's greatness: his approach,
So out of circumstance and sudden, tells us
'Tis not a visitation framed, but forced
By need and accident. What train?

What does he want? He has not come
in a way which matches his father's greatness:
coming so suddenly out of the blue like this tells me
this visit was not planned, but forced
through need and circumstance. What entourage has
he brought?

Gentleman

But few,
And those but mean.

LEONTES
His princess, say you, with him?

Gentleman
Ay, the most peerless piece of earth, I think,
That e'er the sun shone bright on.

PAULINA
O Hermione,
As every present time doth boast itself
Above a better gone, so must thy grave
Give way to what's seen now! Sir, you yourself

Have said and writ so, but your writing now
Is colder than that theme, 'She had not been,
Nor was not to be equall'd;'--thus your verse
Flow'd with her beauty once: 'tis shrewdly ebb'd,
To say you have seen a better.

Gentleman
Pardon, madam:
The one I have almost forgot,--your pardon,--
The other, when she has obtain'd your eye,
Will have your tongue too. This is a creature,
Would she begin a sect, might quench the zeal
Of all professors else, make proselytes
Of who she but bid follow.

PAULINA
How! not women?

Gentleman
Women will love her, that she is a woman
More worth than any man; men, that she is

The rarest of all women.

LEONTES
Go, Cleomenes;
Yourself, assisted with your honour'd friends,
Bring them to our embracement. Still, 'tis strange

Exeunt CLEOMENES and others
He thus should steal upon us.

Only a few,
and those are lower class.

You say his princess is with him?

Yes, the most wonderful creature, I think,
that ever the sun shone brightly on.

Oh Hermione,
just as every era thinks that it is better
than the better one before, so now you are dead
you must give way to what can be seen now! Sir, you
yourself
said and wrote about her, but your writing now
is as cold as her body, 'She had never been,
and could never be, equalled;'—so your verse
was full of her beauty once: now it's emptied,
if you say you've found better.

I apologise, Madam:
the one I have almost forgotten—forgive me—
the other, once you have seen her,
you will sing her praises too. This is a creature,
who, if she began a religion, could crush the fervour
of all other believers, and make converts
of anyone she asked to follow her.

What? Not women?

Women will love her for being a woman
worth more than any man; men will love her for
being
the most unique of women.

Go, Cleomenes;
with the help of your honoured friends
bring them to me for welcome. Still, it's strange

that he should creep in to me like this.

PAULINA

Had our prince, Jewel of children, seen this hour, he had pair'd Well with this lord: there was not full a month Between their births.	*If our prince,* *the jewel of children, was alive now, he would have made* *a good friend for this lord: there was less than a month* *between their births.*

LEONTES

Prithee, no more; cease; thou know'st He dies to me again when talk'd of: sure, When I shall see this gentleman, thy speeches Will bring me to consider that which may Unfurnish me of reason. They are come.	*Please, no more; stop; you know* *to hear him talked of makes him die again for me: I'm sure,* *that when I see this gentleman, what you said* *will start me thinking about things that* *could drive me mad. Here they are.*

Re-enter CLEOMENES and others, with FLORIZEL and PERDITA

Your mother was most true to wedlock, prince; For she did print your royal father off, Conceiving you: were I but twenty-one, Your father's image is so hit in you, His very air, that I should call you brother, As I did him, and speak of something wildly By us perform'd before. Most dearly welcome! And your fair princess,--goddess!--O, alas! I lost a couple, that 'twixt heaven and earth Might thus have stood begetting wonder as You, gracious couple, do: and then I lost-- All mine own folly--the society, Amity too, of your brave father, whom, Though bearing misery, I desire my life Once more to look on him.	*Your mother was a very faithful wife, prince;* *for when she conceived you she made a perfect* *copy of your royal father. If I was just twenty-one,* *you are so identical to your father* *in every way that I would call you brother,* *as I called him, and speak with excitement about things* *we had done before. You are most warmly welcome!* *And your lovely Princess,--Goddess!--Oh, alas!* *I have lost two who could have stood* *in this world like you two, causing amazement* *as you do: and then I lost--* *all through my own stupidity--the company* *and friendship also of your brave father, whom* *I want to go on living, though my life is miserable,* *to see again.*

FLORIZEL

By his command Have I here touch'd Sicilia and from him Give you all greetings that a king, at friend, Can send his brother: and, but infirmity Which waits upon worn times hath something seized His wish'd ability, he had himself The lands and waters 'twixt your throne and his Measured to look upon you; whom he loves-- He bade me say so--more than all the sceptres And those that bear them living.	*It is at his orders* *that I have come to Sicily and from him* *I give you all the greetings that a king, a friend,* *can send to his brother: and, but for the fact that* *illness which comes with age means he can't do* *everything he would like to, he himself* *would have crossed the waters between your countries* *to see you whom he loves--* *he told me to say so--more than all the crowns* *or all those living who wear them.*

LEONTES

O my brother,
Good gentleman! the wrongs I have done thee stir
Afresh within me, and these thy offices,
So rarely kind, are as interpreters
Of my behind-hand slackness. Welcome hither,
As is the spring to the earth. And hath he too

Exposed this paragon to the fearful usage,

At least ungentle, of the dreadful Neptune,
To greet a man not worth her pains, much less
The adventure of her person?

Oh my brother,
good gentleman! The wrongs I have done you
rise up within me again, and these messages,
so wonderfully kind, are signposts showing
what I have neglected. You are welcome here
as the spring is welcome to the Earth. And has he also
exposed this model of perfection to the horrible risks,
at the best discomfort, of the dreadful ocean,
to greet a man who is not worth the effort, much less
taking any risks?

FLORIZEL
Good my lord,
She came from Libya.

My good lord,
she came from Libya.

LEONTES
Where the warlike Smalus,
That noble honour'd lord, is fear'd and loved?

Where the warlike Smalus,
that noble honoured lord, is feared and loved?

FLORIZEL
Most royal sir, from thence; from him, whose daughter
His tears proclaim'd his, parting with her: thence,
A prosperous south-wind friendly, we have cross'd,
To execute the charge my father gave me
For visiting your highness: my best train
I have from your Sicilian shores dismiss'd;
Who for Bohemia bend, to signify
Not only my success in Libya, sir,
But my arrival and my wife's in safety
Here where we are.

Your Highness, from there; from him, whose tears
on parting showed she is his daughter: we crossed
from there with a favourable southerly wind
to obey the instructions my father gave me
to visit your Highness: I sent most of my entourage
away from your Sicilian shores;
they are headed for Bohemia, to give news
not only of my success in Libya, sir,
but my and my wife's safe arrival
in this place.

LEONTES
The blessed gods
Purge all infection from our air whilst you
Do climate here! You have a holy father,
A graceful gentleman; against whose person,
So sacred as it is, I have done sin:
For which the heavens, taking angry note,
Have left me issueless; and your father's blest,

As he from heaven merits it, with you
Worthy his goodness. What might I have been,
Might I a son and daughter now have look'd on,

May the blessed gods
strip all disease from our air while you
are stopping here! Your father is a good man,
and a graceful gentleman; I have sinned
against his holy person:
the heavens, seeing this and furious with it,
have left me without an heir; as your father is blessed,
as he deserves reward from heaven, with you,
who match his goodness. What could I have been,
if I had a son and daughter like the ones I look on now,

Such goodly things as you!

such wonderful creatures as you!

Enter a Lord

Lord
Most noble sir,
That which I shall report will bear no credit,
Were not the proof so nigh. Please you, great sir,

Bohemia greets you from himself by me;
Desires you to attach his son, who has--
His dignity and duty both cast off--
Fled from his father, from his hopes, and with
A shepherd's daughter.

Your Highness,
what I have to say will not be believed,
if it wasn't for the fact that proof is coming. Great sir,
Bohemia sends you his greetings through me;
he requests that you arrest his son, who has—
forgetting both his position and his duty—
run away from his father, from his inheritance, with a shepherd's daughter.

LEONTES
Where's Bohemia? speak.

Where is Bohemia? Speak.

Lord
Here in your city; I now came from him:
I speak amazedly; and it becomes
My marvel and my message. To your court
Whiles he was hastening, in the chase, it seems,
Of this fair couple, meets he on the way
The father of this seeming lady and
Her brother, having both their country quitted
With this young prince.

Here in your city; I just came from him:
My excited way of speaking suits
my astonishment and my message. While he was
hurrying to your court, pursuing, it seems,
this fair couple, he met on the way
the father of this apparent lady and
her brother, who had both left their country
with this young prince.

FLORIZEL
Camillo has betray'd me;
Whose honour and whose honesty till now
Endured all weathers.

Camillo has betrayed me;
until now his honour and his honesty
were beyond reproach.

Lord
Lay't so to his charge:
He's with the king your father.

Yes you can blame him:
he is with the king your father.

LEONTES
Who? Camillo?

Who? Camillo?

Lord
Camillo, sir; I spake with him; who now
Has these poor men in question. Never saw I
Wretches so quake: they kneel, they kiss the earth;

Forswear themselves as often as they speak:
Bohemia stops his ears, and threatens them
With divers deaths in death.

Camillo, sir; I spoke to him; he now
is interrogating these poor men. I never saw
wretches shake like them: they kneel, they kiss the earth;
they perjure themselves every time they speak:
Bohemia blocks his ears, and threatens them
with fates worse than death.

PERDITA
O my poor father!
The heaven sets spies upon us, will not have
Our contract celebrated.

LEONTES
You are married?

FLORIZEL
We are not, sir, nor are we like to be;
The stars, I see, will kiss the valleys first:
The odds for high and low's alike.

LEONTES
My lord,
Is this the daughter of a king?

FLORIZEL
She is,
When once she is my wife.

LEONTES
That 'once' I see by your good father's speed
Will come on very slowly. I am sorry,
Most sorry, you have broken from his liking
Where you were tied in duty, and as sorry
Your choice is not so rich in worth as beauty,
That you might well enjoy her.

FLORIZEL
Dear, look up:
Though Fortune, visible an enemy,
Should chase us with my father, power no jot
Hath she to change our loves. Beseech you, sir,
Remember since you owed no more to time
Than I do now: with thought of such affections,
Step forth mine advocate; at your request
My father will grant precious things as trifles.

LEONTES
Would he do so, I'd beg your precious mistress,
Which he counts but a trifle.

PAULINA
Sir, my liege,

Oh my poor father!
The gods have set their spies on us, they don't want
our wedding to be celebrated.

Are you married?

We are not, sir, nor are we likely to be;
I can see the stars will fall into the valleys first:
the odds are the same for her and for me.

My lord,
is this a king's daughter?

She will be,
once she is my wife.

'Once' is not very likely to happen, judging by
your father's actions. I'm sorry,
very sorry, that you have upset the one
whom you should have obeyed, and just as sorry
that your choice is not as noble as she is beautiful,
so that you could definitely enjoy her.

Keep your head up, dear:
although Fortune seems to be our enemy,
chasing us with my father, she hasn't the slightest
power to change our love. I beg you, sir,
remember when you were my age:
thinking of the love you had then,
step up and speak for me; at your request
my father will grant precious things as if they were
worthless.

If he did, I'd ask for your beautiful mistress,
as he thinks she is worthless.

Sir, my lord,

Your eye hath too much youth in't: not a month
'Fore your queen died, she was more worth such
gazes
Than what you look on now.

LEONTES
I thought of her,
Even in these looks I made.

To FLORIZEL
But your petition
Is yet unanswer'd. I will to your father:
Your honour not o'erthrown by your desires,

I am friend to them and you: upon which errand

I now go toward him; therefore follow me
And mark what way I make: come, good my lord.

Exeunt

you look too much at the young: less than a month
before your queen died, she was more deserving of
such looks
than what you are now looking at.

I was thinking of her,
even as I was looking this way.

But I haven't yet answered
your request. I will go to your father:
if your honour has not been damaged by your
desires,
I will be supportive of them and you: I'll go to see
him
on this errand; so follow me
and see how I get on: come, my good lord.

Scene 2

SCENE II. Before LEONTES' palace.

Enter AUTOLYCUS and a Gentleman

AUTOLYCUS
Beseech you, sir, were you present at this relation?

Tell me, sir, were you there when this happened?

First Gentleman
I was by at the opening of the fardel, heard the old

shepherd deliver the manner how he found it:
whereupon, after a little amazedness, we were all
commanded out of the chamber; only this methought I
heard the shepherd say, he found the child.

I was there when the bundle was opened, heard the old
shepherd explain how he had found it:
then, after some confusion, we were all
ordered out of the room; but I thought I heard
the shepherd say, he had found the child.

AUTOLYCUS
I would most gladly know the issue of it.

I would very much like to know how this turned out.

First Gentleman
I make a broken delivery of the business; but the
changes I perceived in the king and Camillo were
very notes of admiration: they seemed almost, with
staring on one another, to tear the cases of their
eyes; there was speech in their dumbness, language

in their very gesture; they looked as they had heard

of a world ransomed, or one destroyed: a notable

passion of wonder appeared in them; but the wisest

beholder, that knew no more but seeing, could not
say if the importance were joy or sorrow; but in the
extremity of the one, it must needs be.

I can't give you all the details; but I saw
that the King and Camillo were
absolutely astonished: they seemed almost, as
they looked at each other, as if their eyes would
pop out of their heads; their silence spoke volumes,
their
gestures were like speech; they looked as if they had
heard
of a world they thought had been stolen or
destroyed:you could see
that they were absolutely astonished; but the
cleverest
observer, if he was only watching, could not say
if joy or sorrow was uppermost; but it must
have been the strongest of one of those.

Enter another Gentleman
Here comes a gentleman that haply knows more.
The news, Rogero?

Second Gentleman
Nothing but bonfires: the oracle is fulfilled; the

king's daughter is found: such a deal of wonder is

It is all celebrations: the Oracle has been fulfilled;
the
kings daughter has been found: such amazing things

broken out within this hour that ballad-makers
cannot be able to express it.
Enter a third Gentleman

Here comes the Lady Paulina's steward: he can
deliver you more. How goes it now, sir? this news
which is called true is so like an old tale, that
the verity of it is in strong suspicion: has the king
found his heir?

Third Gentleman
Most true, if ever truth were pregnant by
circumstance: that which you hear you'll swear you
see, there is such unity in the proofs. The mantle
of Queen Hermione's, her jewel about the neck of it,
the letters of Antigonus found with it which they
know to be his character, the majesty of the
creature in resemblance of the mother, the affection
of nobleness which nature shows above her breeding,
and many other evidences proclaim her with all
certainty to be the king's daughter. Did you see
the meeting of the two kings?

Second Gentleman
No.

Third Gentleman
Then have you lost a sight, which was to be seen,
cannot be spoken of. There might you have beheld
one
joy crown another, so and in such manner that it
seemed sorrow wept to take leave of them, for their
joy waded in tears. There was casting up of eyes,

holding up of hands, with countenances of such
distraction that they were to be known by garment,

not by favour. Our king, being ready to leap out of
himself for joy of his found daughter, as if that
joy were now become a loss, cries 'O, thy mother,

thy mother!' then asks Bohemia forgiveness; then

embraces his son-in-law; then again worries he his
daughter with clipping her; now he thanks the old
shepherd, which stands by like a weather-bitten

conduit of many kings' reigns. I never heard of such

---

*have happened in this hour that ballad makers
will not be able to do it justice.*

*Here is the Lady Paulina's steward: he can
tell you more. What's happening now, sir? This news
which they say is true is so like some legend that
the truth of it is called into question: has the king
found his heir?*

*It's very true, if truth was ever proved by
evidence: you will believe it when you
see it, the evidence all hangs together. The robe
of Queen Hermione, with her jewel around its neck,
the letters of Antigonus found with it in
his handwriting, the majesty of the
creature who looks exactly like the mother, the air
of nobility which nature shows above her breeding,
and many other proofs declare her absolutely
definitely the King's daughter. Did you see
the meeting of the two kings?*

No.

*Then you missed an indescribable sight.
You would have seen one happiness*

*on top of another, in such a way that it
seemed that sorrow wept to leave them, for their
joy was drowned in tears. There was a rolling of
eyes,
holding up of hands, with faces so
contorted that they could only be known by their
clothes,
not their appearance. Our king, being beside
himself with joy at finding his daughter, as if that joy
had now become a loss, cried, 'oh, your mother,
your
mother!' Then he asked Bohemia for forgiveness;
then embraced
his son-in-law; then again he ruffled his
daughter by hugging her; now he thanked the old
shepherd, who was standing by, like a
weatherbeaten
gargoyle which had seen many kings' reigns. I never*

another encounter, which lames report to follow it

and undoes description to do it.

heard of such
a meeting, which cannot be imagined from hearing
about it,
it was indescribable.

Second Gentleman
What, pray you, became of Antigonus, that carried
hence the child?

Tell me, what became of Antigonus, who carried
the child there?

Third Gentleman
Like an old tale still, which will have matter to
rehearse, though credit be asleep and not an ear
open. He was torn to pieces with a bear: this
avouches the shepherd's son; who has not only his
innocence, which seems much, to justify him, but a
handkerchief and rings of his that Paulina knows.

It's still like a legend, which still has things to say
even when nobody believes it or is even listening.
He was torn to pieces by a bear: this
is sworn to by the shepherd's son; he is backed up
not only by his innocence, which seems great, but a
handkerchief and rings of his that Paulina
recognised.

First Gentleman
What became of his bark and his followers?

What happened to his ship and his followers?

Third Gentleman
Wrecked the same instant of their master's death
and
in the view of the shepherd: so that all the
instruments which aided to expose the child were
even then lost when it was found. But O, the noble
combat that 'twixt joy and sorrow was fought in
Paulina! She had one eye declined for the loss of
her husband, another elevated that the oracle was

fulfilled: she lifted the princess from the earth,
and so locks her in embracing, as if she would pin
her to her heart that she might no more be in danger
of losing.

It was wrecked at the same time as their master died,

the shepherd saw it: so all the
things which conspired to expose the child were
lost at the moment it was found. But oh, what a
noble battle Paulina fought between joy and
sorrow. She had one eye cast down at the loss of
her husband, another raised up because the Oracle
was
fulfilled: she lifted the princess off the ground
and hugged her so tight, it was as if she wanted
to pin her to her heart so that she could never
lose her again.

First Gentleman
The dignity of this act was worth the audience of
kings and princes; for by such was it acted.

The beauty of this act was worthy of its audience of
kings and princes; because it was played out by
them.

Third Gentleman
One of the prettiest touches of all and that which
angled for mine eyes, caught the water though not
the fish, was when, at the relation of the queen's
death, with the manner how she came to't bravely
confessed and lamented by the king, how

One of the prettiest touches of all, and the one which
caught my eye, pulling the water out if not
the fish, was when, at the story of the queen's
death, with the manner of how it happened being
honestly confessed and lamented by the king, how

attentiveness wounded his daughter; till, from one
sign of dolour to another, she did, with an 'Alas,'
I would fain say, bleed tears, for I am sure my
heart wept blood. Who was most marble there
changed
colour; some swooned, all sorrowed: if all the world
could have seen 't, the woe had been universal.

*hearing it wounded his daughter; until, between
one sad sigh and another she said, 'Alas,'
and did, I would say, bleed tears, for I am sure my
heart wept blood. The hardest people changed
colour; some fainted, all lamented: if everybody
could have seen it, the whole world would be
sorrowing.*

First Gentleman
Are they returned to the court?

Have they gone back to the court?

Third Gentleman
No: the princess hearing of her mother's statue,

*No: when the princess heard about her mother's
statue,*

which is in the keeping of Paulina,--a piece many
years in doing and now newly performed by that rare
Italian master, Julio Romano, who, had he himself
eternity and could put breath into his work, would
beguile Nature of her custom, so perfectly he is her

*which Paulina has--a piece which took many
years to complete, only just finished by that amazing
Italian master, Julio Romano, who, if he had
eternity and could make his works breathe, would
put Nature out of business, he copies her so
perfectly:*

ape: he so near to Hermione hath done Hermione that
they say one would speak to her and stand in hope
of
answer: thither with all greediness of affection

*he has made such a perfect image of Hermione that
they say that one would speak to her and wait
expecting
an answer: so they have gone there with the
eagerness of love*

are they gone, and there they intend to sup.

intending to drink their fill.

Second Gentleman
I thought she had some great matter there in hand;

*I thought she had some great business going on
there;*

for she hath privately twice or thrice a day, ever
since the death of Hermione, visited that removed
house. Shall we thither and with our company piece
the rejoicing?

*for she has, alone, two or three times a day, ever
since the death of Hermione, visited that isolated
building. Shall we go there and add our company
to the rejoicing?*

First Gentleman
Who would be thence that has the benefit of access?
every wink of an eye some new grace will be born:
our absence makes us unthrifty to our knowledge.
Let's along.

*Who wouldn't be there if they were allowed in?
Some new beauty seems to happen every second:
not being there means we're missing out.
Let's go.*

Exeunt Gentlemen

AUTOLYCUS
Now, had I not the dash of my former life in me,

*Now, if I didn't have the taint of my former life on
me,*

would preferment drop on my head. I brought the old

promotion would come my way. I brought the old

man and his son aboard the prince: told him I heard
them talk of a fardel and I know not what: but he
at that time, overfond of the shepherd's daughter,
so he then took her to be, who began to be much
sea-sick, and himself little better, extremity of
weather continuing, this mystery remained
undiscovered. But 'tis all one to me; for had I
been the finder out of this secret, it would not
have relished among my other discredits.

Enter Shepherd and Clown
Here come those I have done good to against my will,
and already appearing in the blossoms of their fortune.

Shepherd
Come, boy; I am past moe children, but thy sons and
daughters will be all gentlemen born.

Clown
You are well met, sir. You denied to fight with me
this other day, because I was no gentleman born.
See you these clothes? say you see them not and
think me still no gentleman born: you were best say
these robes are not gentlemen born: give me the
lie, do, and try whether I am not now a gentleman
born.
AUTOLYCUS

I know you are now, sir, a gentleman born.

Clown
Ay, and have been so any time these four hours.

Shepherd
And so have I, boy.

Clown
So you have: but I was a gentleman born before my

---

man and his son to the prince's ship: I told him I heard
them talk of a bundle and goodness knows what else: but he
at that time, too concerned with the shepherd's daughter,
as he then thought she was, who began to be very seasick, and he wasn't much better, with the bad weather carrying on, this mystery was not investigated. But it's all the same to me; if I had discovered the secret, it wouldn't have outweighed all my other black marks.

Here come the ones I have helped without meaning to,
their appearance shows they've already gone up in the world.

Come, boy; I'm past child-rearing age, but your sons and
daughters will all be born gentlemen.

I'm glad to meet you, sir. You refused to fight with me
the other day, because I was not born a gentleman.
Do you see these clothes? You can't look at them and still say I am not a born gentleman: you might just as well
say these robes are not born gentlemen: lie to me now, go on, and see if I am not a born gentleman.

I know you have now, sir, become a born gentleman.

Yes, and I have been for the last four hours.

And so have I, boy.

Yes you have: but I was a born gentleman before my

father; for the king's son took me by the hand, and

called me brother; and then the two kings called my

father brother; and then the prince my brother and
the princess my sister called my father father; and
so we wept, and there was the first gentleman-like
tears that ever we shed.

Shepherd
We may live, son, to shed many more.

Clown
Ay; or else 'twere hard luck, being in so
preposterous estate as we are.

AUTOLYCUS
I humbly beseech you, sir, to pardon me all the
faults I have committed to your worship and to give
me your good report to the prince my master.

Shepherd
Prithee, son, do; for we must be gentle, now we are

gentlemen.

Clown
Thou wilt amend thy life?

AUTOLYCUS
Ay, an it like your good worship.

Clown
Give me thy hand: I will swear to the prince thou

art as honest a true fellow as any is in Bohemia.

Shepherd
You may say it, but not swear it.

Clown
Not swear it, now I am a gentleman? Let boors and
franklins say it, I'll swear it.

Shepherd
How if it be false, son?

Clown

father; because the king's son took me by the hand, and
called me his brother; and then the two kings called my
father brother; and then the prince my brother and
the princess my sister called my father father; and
so we wept, and those were the first gentlemanly
tears that we ever shed.

We may live, son, to shed many more.

Yes, or else we would be very unlucky, seeing
the preposterous state we're in.

I humbly beg you, sir, to forgive me all the
wrongs I have done your worship and to give
a good report of me to the prince my master.

Please do this, son; for we must be gentle, now we are
gentlemen.

You will change your lifestyle?

Yes, if it pleases your good worship.

Give me your hand: I will swear to the Prince that you
are as honest a loyal fellow as anyone in Bohemia.

You can say it, but don't swear it.

Not swear it, now I'm a gentleman? Let peasants and
yeomen say it, I shall swear it.

What if it turns out to be false, son?

If it be ne'er so false, a true gentleman may swear
it in the behalf of his friend: and I'll swear to
the prince thou art a tall fellow of thy hands and
that thou wilt not be drunk; but I know thou art no

tall fellow of thy hands and that thou wilt be
drunk: but I'll swear it, and I would thou wouldst
be a tall fellow of thy hands.

AUTOLYCUS
I will prove so, sir, to my power.

Clown
Ay, by any means prove a tall fellow: if I do not

wonder how thou darest venture to be drunk, not
being a tall fellow, trust me not. Hark! the kings
and the princes, our kindred, are going to see the
queen's picture. Come, follow us: we'll be thy

good masters.

Exeunt

*However false it is, a true gentleman may swear
to it on behalf of a friend: and I'll swear to
the prince that you are a good and brave man
and that you won't get drunk; although I know you
are not
a good and brave man and that you will get
drunk: but I'll swear to it, and I want you to be
a good and brave man.*

I'll do the best I can, sir.

*Yes, do anything you can to show you're a good
fellow: if I do not
wonder how you can dare to get drunk, if you're not
a good fellow, don't trust me. Listen! The kings
and the princes, our relatives, are going to see the
image of the queen. Come on, follow us: we will be
your
good masters.*

Scene 3

SCENE III. A chapel in PAULINA'S house.

Enter LEONTES, POLIXENES, FLORIZEL, PERDITA, CAMILLO, PAULINA, Lords, and Attendants

LEONTES
O grave and good Paulina, the great comfort
That I have had of thee!

*O wise and good Paulina, what great comfort
I have had from you!*

PAULINA
What, sovereign sir,
I did not well I meant well. All my services
You have paid home: but that you have vouchsafed,
With your crown'd brother and these your contracted
Heirs of your kingdoms, my poor house to visit,
It is a surplus of your grace, which never
My life may last to answer.

*Your highness,
when I did wrong I meant well. You have repaid
all my services: but that you have condescended,
with your crowned brother and these
heirs to your kingdoms, to visit my poor house,
is a great overpayment of kindness
which I can never live long enough to repay.*

LEONTES
O Paulina,
We honour you with trouble: but we came
To see the statue of our queen: your gallery
Have we pass'd through, not without much content

In many singularities; but we saw not
That which my daughter came to look upon,
The statue of her mother.

*Oh Paulina,
we are only giving you trouble: but I came
to see the statue of my queen: we have
walked through your gallery, and been very
impressed
with the things you have; but we did not see
the thing which my daughter came to look at,
the statue of her mother.*

PAULINA
As she lived peerless,
So her dead likeness, I do well believe,
Excels whatever yet you look'd upon
Or hand of man hath done; therefore I keep it
Lonely, apart. But here it is: prepare
To see the life as lively mock'd as ever
Still sleep mock'd death: behold, and say 'tis well.

*As she had no match in life,
I certainly believe that her dead image
is greater than anything you have ever seen
or that man has ever created; so I keep it
apart in isolation. But here it is: prepare
to see life imitated as well
as sleep ever imitated death: look, and say it is
good.*

PAULINA draws a curtain, and discovers HERMIONE standing like a statue
I like your silence, it the more shows off
Your wonder: but yet speak; first, you, my liege,
Comes it not something near?

*I like your silence, it demonstrates
your amazement: but now speak; first you, my lord,
isn't it pretty lifelike?*

LEONTES

Her natural posture!	*That's just how she was!*
Chide me, dear stone, that I may say indeed	*Scold me, dear stone, so that I can truly say*
Thou art Hermione; or rather, thou art she	*you are Hermione; though actually you are*
In thy not chiding, for she was as tender	*like her in not scolding, for she was as kind*
As infancy and grace. But yet, Paulina,	*as a child, as a god. But yet, Paulina,*
Hermione was not so much wrinkled, nothing	*Hermione did not have as many wrinkles, she was not*
So aged as this seems.	*as old as this seems to be.*

POLIXENES

O, not by much.	*Certainly not.*

PAULINA

So much the more our carver's excellence;	*This just shows how excellent the sculptor is;*
Which lets go by some sixteen years and makes her	*he has let sixteen years go by and makes her*
As she lived now.	*as if she were alive today.*

LEONTES

As now she might have done,	*As she could have been,*
So much to my good comfort, as it is	*which would have been so good for me*
Now piercing to my soul. O, thus she stood,	*that it is now stabbing at my soul. Oh, this is how she stood,*
Even with such life of majesty, warm life,	*with such a queenly life in her, warm life,*
As now it coldly stands, when first I woo'd her!	*that now stands cold, when I first wooed her!*
I am ashamed: does not the stone rebuke me	*I am ashamed: isn't the stone rebuking me*
For being more stone than it? O royal piece,	*for being more stone than it? Oh royal sculpture,*
There's magic in thy majesty, which has	*there's magic in your majesty, which has*
My evils conjured to remembrance and	*reminded me of my sins and*
From thy admiring daughter took the spirits,	*taken all the spirit out of your admiring daughter,*
Standing like stone with thee.	*who stands like stone like you.*

PERDITA

And give me leave,	*And give me permission,*
And do not say 'tis superstition, that	*and don't say that it is superstitious, to*
I kneel and then implore her blessing. Lady,	*kneel and beg for her blessing. Lady,*
Dear queen, that ended when I but began,	*dear queen, who died when I was born,*
Give me that hand of yours to kiss.	*give me that hand of yours to kiss.*

PAULINA

O, patience!	*Oh, be careful!*
The statue is but newly fix'd, the colour's not dry.	*The statue has just been painted, the colour's not dry.*

CAMILLO

My lord, your sorrow was too sore laid on,	*My lord, the sorrow you had was too great,*
Which sixteen winters cannot blow away,	*sixteen winters could not blow it away,*

So many summers dry; scarce any joy

Did ever so long live; no sorrow
But kill'd itself much sooner.

POLIXENES
Dear my brother,
Let him that was the cause of this have power
To take off so much grief from you as he
Will piece up in himself.

PAULINA
Indeed, my lord,
If I had thought the sight of my poor image
Would thus have wrought you,--for the stone is
mine--
I'ld not have show'd it.

LEONTES
Do not draw the curtain.

PAULINA
No longer shall you gaze on't, lest your fancy

May think anon it moves.

LEONTES
Let be, let be.
Would I were dead, but that, methinks, already--
What was he that did make it? See, my lord,
Would you not deem it breathed? and that those
veins
Did verily bear blood?

POLIXENES
Masterly done:
The very life seems warm upon her lip.

LEONTES
The fixture of her eye has motion in't,
As we are mock'd with art.

PAULINA
I'll draw the curtain:
My lord's almost so far transported that
He'll think anon it lives.

*the same number of summers could not dry it;
there's hardly any joy
that ever lived for so long; no sorrow
that didn't die earlier.*

*My dear brother,
let the one who was the cause of this
take as much of the burden of grief from you as he
can take upon himself.*

*Indeed, my lord,
if I'd thought the sight of my poor sculpture
would have had this effect on you--for the stone is
mine--
I wouldn't have showed it to you.*

Don't draw the curtain.

*You shall look at it any more, in case your
imagination
starts to think that it's moving.*

*Let it be, let it be.
I wish I were dead, except that, I think, already--
who was the person who made this? See, my lord,
wouldn't you think that it's breathing? And that those
veins
are really full of blood?*

*Masterfully done:
her lips look as though they actually had the warmth
of life in them.*

*Her eyeballs seem to move,
as we are tricked by art.*

*I'll draw the curtain:
my lord is so carried away that
he'll soon be thinking it's alive.*

LEONTES
O sweet Paulina,
Make me to think so twenty years together!
No settled senses of the world can match
The pleasure of that madness. Let 't alone.

Oh sweet Paulina,
let me think that for twenty years at a stretch!
No sensible pleasures of the world can match
the pleasure of that madness. Leave it be.

PAULINA
I am sorry, sir, I have thus far stirr'd you: but
I could afflict you farther.

I'm sorry, sir, to have agitated you so much: but
I could do more.

LEONTES
Do, Paulina;
For this affliction has a taste as sweet
As any cordial comfort. Still, methinks,
There is an air comes from her: what fine chisel
Could ever yet cut breath? Let no man mock me,

For I will kiss her.

Do, Paulina;
for this illness tastes as sweet
as any health giving cordial. Still, I think
that air is coming from her: what fine chisel
has ever been able to sculpt breath? Nobody should
mock me,
I am going to kiss her.

PAULINA
Good my lord, forbear:
The ruddiness upon her lip is wet;
You'll mar it if you kiss it, stain your own
With oily painting. Shall I draw the curtain?

My good lord, don't do it:
the red on her lips is wet;
you'll spoil it if you kiss it, and stain your own
with oil paint. Shall I draw the curtain?

LEONTES
No, not these twenty years.

No, not for twenty years.

PERDITA
So long could I
Stand by, a looker on.

That's how long I could
stand by, watching.

PAULINA
Either forbear,
Quit presently the chapel, or resolve you
For more amazement. If you can behold it,
I'll make the statue move indeed, descend
And take you by the hand; but then you'll think--
Which I protest against--I am assisted
By wicked powers.

Either stop,
and leave the chapel at once, or prepare
for more amazement. If you can bear it,
I will indeed make the statue move, climb down
and take you by the hand; but then you'll think—
which I tell you I'm not—that I am assisted
by wicked powers.

LEONTES
What you can make her do,
I am content to look on: what to speak,
I am content to hear; for 'tis as easy
To make her speak as move.

Whatever you can make her do,
I am happy to see: whatever you can make her say,
I am happy to hear; for it would be as easy
to make her speak as to make her move.

PAULINA

It is required
You do awake your faith. Then all stand still;
Or- those that think it is unlawful business
I am about, let them depart.

You must
have faith. You must all stand still;
anyone who thinks that I am about
to do something sinful, let them leave.

LEONTES
Proceed:
No foot shall stir.

Carry on:
no one will move an inch.

PAULINA
Music, awake her; strike!

Music, wake her up; now!

Music
'Tis time; descend; be stone no more; approach;

Strike all that look upon with marvel. Come,
I'll fill your grave up: stir, nay, come away,
Bequeath to death your numbness, for from him
Dear life redeems you. You perceive she stirs:

It's time; come down; no longer be stone; come to
us;
astonish everyone who is watching. Come,
I'll fill up your grave: move, no, come away:
give your numbness back to death; for
dear life saves you from him. You see she's moving:

HERMIONE comes down
Start not; her actions shall be holy as
You hear my spell is lawful: do not shun her
Until you see her die again; for then
You kill her double. Nay, present your hand:
When she was young you woo'd her; now in age
Is she become the suitor?

don't flinch; her actions will be as holy as
my spell is lawful, which you will hear.
Do not reject her
until you see her die again; if you do
you will kill her twice. No, give her your hand:
when she was young you wooed her; now, when she
is old,
has she become the wooer?

LEONTES
O, she's warm!
If this be magic, let it be an art
Lawful as eating.

Oh, she's warm!
If this is magic, let it be an art
as lawful as eating.

POLIXENES
She embraces him.

She is embracing him.

CAMILLO
She hangs about his neck:
If she pertain to life let her speak too.

She has thrown her arms around his neck:
if she is alive let her speak too.

POLIXENES
Ay, and make't manifest where she has lived,
Or how stolen from the dead.

Yes, and explain where she has been living,
or how she has come back from the dead.

PAULINA
That she is living,

That she is alive,

Were it but told you, should be hooted at
Like an old tale: but it appears she lives,
Though yet she speak not. Mark a little while.
Please you to interpose, fair madam: kneel
And pray your mother's blessing. Turn, good lady;
Our Perdita is found.

if you were only told it, you would mock it
like an old story: but you can see she lives,
although she has not yet spoken. Wait a little while.
Please put yourself forward, fair madam: kneel
and beg for your mother's blessing. Turn, good lady;
our Perdita is found.

HERMIONE
You gods, look down
And from your sacred vials pour your graces
Upon my daughter's head! Tell me, mine own.
Where hast thou been preserved? where lived? how
 found
Thy father's court? for thou shalt hear that I,

Knowing by Paulina that the oracle
Gave hope thou wast in being, have preserved
Myself to see the issue.

You gods, look down
and from your sacred urns pour your blessings
upon my daughter's head! Tell me, my own,
where have you been kept? Where have you lived?
How did you
come back to your father's court? For as you shall
hear I,
knowing from Paulina that the Oracle
gave hope that you were alive, have saved
myself to see the result.

PAULINA
There's time enough for that;
Lest they desire upon this push to trouble
Your joys with like relation. Go together,
You precious winners all; your exultation
Partake to every one. I, an old turtle,
Will wing me to some wither'd bough and there
My mate, that's never to be found again,
Lament till I am lost.

There is time enough for that;
we don't want them at this happy moment
to start telling their own stories. Go together,
all you precious winners; share your happiness
with everyone. I, an old turtledove,
will fly to some dead branch and there
I will sing sad songs for my mate,
who will never be found again,
until I am dead.

LEONTES
O, peace, Paulina!
Thou shouldst a husband take by my consent,
As I by thine a wife: this is a match,
And made between's by vows. Thou hast found
mine;
But how, is to be question'd; for I saw her,
As I thought, dead, and have in vain said many
A prayer upon her grave. I'll not seek far--
For him, I partly know his mind--to find thee
An honourable husband. Come, Camillo,
And take her by the hand, whose worth and honesty
Is richly noted and here justified
By us, a pair of kings. Let's from this place.
What! look upon my brother: both your pardons,

That e'er I put between your holy looks
My ill suspicion. This is your son-in-law,

Oh, peace, Paulina!
You will take a husband with my permission,
as I take a wife with yours: this is a bargain
that we have sworn between us. You have found
mine;
but how, I don't know; for I saw her,
as I thought, dead, and have in vain said many
prayers at her grave. I'll not look far–
I partly know what he's thinking–to find you
an honourable husband. Come, Camillo,
and take her by the hand; your worth and honesty
is fully appreciated and vouched for
by us, a pair of kings. Let's go from this place.
What! Look at my brother: both of you
forgive me,
for ever regarding your holy looks
with my foul suspicions. This is your son-in-law,

And son unto the king, who, heavens directing,
Is troth-plight to your daughter. Good Paulina,
Lead us from hence, where we may leisurely
Each one demand an answer to his part
Perform'd in this wide gap of time since first
We were dissever'd: hastily lead away.

Exeunt

the son of the king, who, directed by the gods,
is engaged to your daughter. Good Paulina,
take us from here, where we can at leisure
question each other, and say what has happened
in this great stretch of time, since we
were first separated: quickly take us away.

CPSIA information can be obtained
at www.ICGtesting.com
Printed in the USA
LVHW062154270421
685787LV00023B/577